Melinda Rankin

Twenty Years Among the Mexicans

A narrative of missionary labor

Melinda Rankin

Twenty Years Among the Mexicans
A narrative of missionary labor

ISBN/EAN: 9783743351820

Manufactured in Europe, USA, Canada, Australia, Japa

Cover: Foto ©ninafisch / pixelio.de

Manufactured and distributed by brebook publishing software (www.brebook.com)

Melinda Rankin

Twenty Years Among the Mexicans

PREFACE.

THE narrative is written, and I have concluded to give it to the public. It was commenced under very serious doubts as to the propriety of its publication, lest there might appear a spirit of egotism in arraying my imperfect labors before the world. In gathering up and writing out the actual facts of my personal experience, I have found much satisfaction. The review of the way in which the Lord has led me has greatly strengthened my faith in His providential dealings with His people, and confirmed my belief that He still accomplishes His divine purposes through weak instrumentalities. In view of this, I have arrived at the conclusion that the facts of my personal missionary experience are not my own, and therefore I have no right to suppress them, however much my natural disposition may incline me to do so. Hence, I give this brief narrative of my Twenty Years' Experience among the Mexicans, to the public, from a firm conviction of duty to God, and will indulge the hope that He will make it useful to those into whose hands the little book may fall.

I am aware it will be subject to various criticisms. With some, it will, I doubt not, be received as an exhibition of God's faithfulness to His promises, and an example of His condescension in favoring one of his weakest servants. If this appreciation be arrived at, I shall be fully compensated for this presentation of my life-service for the Master.

There is another class who may probably deign to look into the book, and who, having no proper understanding of a work of faith, will pronounce the facts presented the result of a wild fanaticism and of a weak and misguided mind. From this class, I most frankly acknowledge, I have expected naught but disapprobation, therefore I shall not be disappointed in any criticisms they may see fit to make.

Then, there are those who profess to have an appreciation and knowledge of missionary labor who may say the work described might have been done better. To such, I would say, I wish you had come into the field at the stage of progress which I entered it, and accomplished the work as you think it ought to have been done. It is quite easy to criticise the labors of predecessors, without due regard to the stupendous disadvantages under which they have labored, and because things have not been brought to a stage of perfection, to say there is an evident failure in their plans and purposes. It is a doubtful question, however, whether these critics could have done better under the same difficult circumstances.

Breaking up the ground and sowing the seed always precedes the harvest. The forest has to be leveled and much hard labor has to be accomplished before towns and cities can be built; and if some of my successors do not find the cities already built, they will at least find some degree of foundation upon which to build.

When I transferred the mission of Northern Mexico to the A. B. C. F. M., I claimed only that a FOUNDATION had been laid, and that the superstructure had yet to be reared. Although there were six organized churches, with some hundreds of converted Mexicans, and a school attached to each church, with a training school for boys in the seminary building in Monterey, also an abundance of precious seed scattered over the land, yet I presented the field as very needy and in great want of efficient laborers for *perfecting this* work, and for fully carrying out the plans and purposes which had been laid in faith and prayer. May God enable those who take up this work to rightly understand it, and give due honor to the agencies which have preceded them.

The gathering of those churches has been done mainly through the instrumentality of native Christians. With the experience which they had gained of the gospel of Christ, they were enabled to reach the hearts of their fellow-countrymen with the same blessed truths far more successfully than any foreign missionary who might have been brought upon the field could have done. There are peculiarities of Mexican mind and character which foreigners fail to understand or reach. Many, *very many*, of the blinded votaries of the papacy in Mexico have been brought to the knowledge of the truth as it is in Jesus through the instructions imparted them by these unlettered Bible readers. To undervalue and set at naught this heaven-approved instrumentality I can not but regard as a sin against the Holy Ghost. To those who lightly estimates these labors, I say, with tearful eyes, be careful in your judgment, lest the Master who called them into His service, and has so significantly accepted this service, be wounded in the house of his professed friends.

Also, I would say to all whom it may concern, that in giving this brief history of my mission among the Mexicans, I have most strenuously endeavored to avoid appropriating undue honor to myself. I have felt it an imperative duty, and it has been my pleasure, to recognize the labors done by others on the field, and to duly notice those labors as far as was consistent with the brevity of my narrative. After I carried my mission into Mexico in 1865, I worked mainly through others, employing both American and native laborers, sometimes having fifteen at a time in the various departments of the field, and being obliged often to leave the work in the charge of suitable persons to come to the United States to solicit the funds for their support. This work I claimed for the American and Foreign Christian Union, and under whose auspices I planted this first mission in Northern Mexico. No other missionary society entered this field until 1870, at which time the Baptist Home Missionary Society employed their first laborer, Rev. Thomas Westrup. In 1871, the Friends sent a missionary to the State of Tamaulipas. In 1872, the Presbyterian Board of Missions sent their first missionaries to the State of Zacatecas, and also to the City of Mexico. In 1873, the Methodist Board

of Missions sent Rev. Dr. Butler to the City of
Mexico. The Episcopalians have a mission in
Mexico, but I am not fully acquainted with the
facts of its origin, or of the date of its commencement. Probably Rev. Mr. Riley, who is an Episcopalian, has transferred his mission in the City of
Mexico to that denomination—am not positive.

If, in my representations, I have made any mistakes, I will most cheerfully rectify those mistakes
when convinced that such have been made.

That this little book shall be an exponent of
truth and justice has been my chief desire and aim;
and that God will bless it as it goes forth to the
public is my most earnest prayer.

MELINDA RANKIN.

CONTENTS.

Twenty Years Among the Mexicans.

CHAPTER I.

Why this book was written—The question of woman's **proper** sphere fully decided—A consecration **to missions**—Patient waiting.

SINCE the failure **of my** health has compelled me to retire from active service on the field, the question has been repeatedly asked me, "Why do you not write a history of your mission among the Mexicans?" Various considerations, having weight in my own mind, at first repelled such an idea, and I uniformly replied, "I am utterly opposed to autobiographies. And it savors too much of egotism for me to set forth to the public my own personal labors. Besides, I do not claim very wonderful displays of magnanimity in any thing I have done. Therefore I am not at all disposed to put my deeds in print, as if I believed them deserving of especial admiration and praise."

The question, however, has continued to be repeated, and that by persons to whose opinion I owed respect. One reverend divine, whom I met for the first time, said to me, "You owe the Christian public a narrative of the way in which God has led you. Your work among the Mexicans has been, most emphatically, the Lord's work, and it seems to me He claims that it should be displayed for His name's sake."

This was a new view of the subject, and I felt constrained to take the matter into serious consideration. Could God be glorified in the effort, I felt willing to take up the cross—for such it seemed to me—and to write out the simple facts connected with my work among the Mexicans. And if, in now giving the details as they come up in my memory, the glory of God shall appear to be the paramount object, I shall probably lay them before the public; but should I discover the motive to be self-glorification, I shall, most unhesitatingly, commit the manuscript to the flames.

One very important consideration which inspires me to this undertaking is the hope that I may prove, by actual facts which have occurred in one woman's life, that our Divine Master has still work for woman to do in His kingdom on earth. When we look into the New Testament we see the important service rendered Him by woman; and we notice also that He not only recognized it, but highly commended it. In relation to an act performed by woman He said, "Wherever the gospel is preached throughout the whole world, this that this woman has done shall be spoken of as a memorial of her." To a very great extent the prevailing sentiment among Christ's people has been, that woman's work should be necessarily circumscribed, lest she transcend the delicacy belonging to her sex. To unwomanly aspirations or conduct I am as much opposed as any one. But had public sentiment been my guide some forty years ago, I should probably have settled down in my New England home with the belief that it was highly improper for me to undertake any signal enterprise for the advancement of Christ's kingdom. But when the light of the glorious Gospel of the Son of God shone into my heart the desire for its extension throughout the whole world took entire possession of me. Impressed with the responsibility of being a redeemed sinner, I wondered how I was to find vent for the boundless aspirations which possessed my whole being, and I almost rebelled against the will of my heavenly Father at the limited sphere which He seemed to have allotted me. In this unquiet frame, I providentially came across the chapter in Paul's Epistle to the Corinthians in which he says, "But now hath God set the members every one of them in the body, as it hath pleased him. And if they were all one member, where were the body? But now are they many members, yet but one body. And the eye can not say unto the hand, I have no need of thee: nor again the head to the feet, I have no need of you. Nay, much more those members of the body, which seem to be more feeble,

2

are necessary." I immediately came to the conclusion that, as a member of Christ's body, although a feeble one, I had a mission to fulfill,
and one sufficiently ample for occupying all the
powers of the body and soul. I felt no proscrip-
tion on account of my sex; nay, I could, and *did*,
adopt the noble sentiment of the lamented Ev-
arts, Secretary of the American Board of Missions,
who was removed by death soon after his appointment. In the acceptance of the responsible position, he writes: "Henceforth, if it please Him, I
am to consecrate myself—my soul and body and
all I have—to a direct effort to execute, in union
with others, the last command of the ascended
Saviour."

CHAPTER II.

What wilt Thou have me to do?—My labors must be beyond
the bounds of New England—Wants of the Valley of the
Mississippi—Two years in Kentucky; thence to the State
of Mississippi—Delighted with the "Sunny South"—Must
divest myself of love of place merely from its worldly attractions.

MY Master, I felt assured, accepted this consecration which, from my heart, I had thus made,
and from thenceforth I regarded myself pledged
to perform such work as He might assign me.   I
was impressed that my mission would be among
the needy and destitute; consequently beyond the
bounds of New England.   From the period of this
consecration a series of trials commenced which
seemed especially appointed by God to test the
sincerity and depth of my motives.   The Master,
I felt assured, was trying my spirit as silver is
tried, in order to prepare me for some special
work.   With the full conviction that in due time
my life's mission would be shown me, I endeavored to "be faithful over the few things," and ap-
plied myself with earnest devotion to a thorough
preparation, and also to teaching the young, both
in Sabbath and week-day schools.   During those
years of waiting and preparing, at intervals would
light from heaven shine upon my pathway as upon

some of old. With the unmistakable aptness of the language of inspiration would these words come unto me: "Fear not, I have called thee by thy name;" "Thou art mine." Oftentimes would I be impressed with this command: "Get thee out of thy country, and from thy kindred, and come into the land which I will show you." When motives stronger than life urged me to remain in my dear New England, the sentiment of the Apostle would impress me with irresistible force: "Necessity is laid upon me; yea, woe is unto me" if I go not to the needy and destitute. Divine grace finally prevailed, and duty impelled me to take the advance step towards my appointed work. I scarcely knew what it was to be, yet I endeavored "to set the Lord before me;" "and because He was at my right hand," I knew I should be guided aright. At that time there was a great call for missionary teachers to go to the Valley of the Mississippi. In consequence of European emigration, Roman Catholicism was fast gaining ground in that portion of country, and urgent appeals were made by American Protestantism for counteracting influences. Under the all-inspiring conviction of duty, with steadfast, yet cheerful purpose, I bade adieu to my New England home and friends, and took up my way toward the West, going as far as Kentucky, which, at that period (1840), was considered quite a remote region. In this State I found a great need of Christian teachers, and, although it did not seem to be the field which answered my utmost aspirations, yet I remained there nearly two years, establishing schools, and sending on to New England for teachers.   I then went to the State of Mississippi, and in this new move I was conscious of the manifest direction of God, which was clearly shown by the opening of the way, and by the welcome reception which I received from the people of that region.   I could see even there abundance of reason why I should have left our highly favored New England, to fill a position so needy as the one which I was called immediately to occupy.

The beautiful "Sunny South," with its highly cultivated and refined society, charmed me, and I fain would have made a permanent residence amid its delightful scenes; but often would the startling question sound in my ears, "What doest thou here, Elijah?" and I would arouse to the consciousness that I was on enchanted ground, and that I must divest myself of love of place merely from its worldly attractions.

CHAPTER III.

Looking over into Mexico—A **dark** prospect—Responsibility
of American Christians—Public appeals unavailing—Resolved to go to Mexico—Closed my labors in Mississippi
and started for Mexico—Remarkable Providences—"A
little child shall lead them"—Could not get immediately
into Mexico—Decided to go to Texas—Incidents of travel
—Unpleasant delay on Red River.

THE dark places of the earth seemed to me the
most fitting spot for one who had made a consecration of all to Christ and His cause; but I remained in Mississippi, with some intervals of absence, until 1846, at which time our country was
engaged in war with Mexico. Mississippi was
largely represented in that war, and when it closed
I learned through returned soldiers and officers
much about the moral destitution prevailing among
the people of Mexico. Here, I learned, was a country right upon our border from which the light of
the Bible had been excluded for centuries. Indeed,
a pure Christianity had never penetrated these dark
regions, as all the previous history of Mexico clearly
proved. Upon the advent of the Spanish conquerors of Mexico, Roman Catholicism, with all its idol-
atrous rites, was substituted for paganism. Notwithstanding the assumptions of the Roman system
of religion, it proved fully as demoralizing, and
which, besides its corrupting tendencies, ground

down the poor inoffensive people under the most despotic bondage. This system of religion **had** reigned supreme, under a tyrannical priesthood, for **more** than three hundred years, and its legitimate fruits were fully **apparent by the moral** degradation prevailing throughout **one of the** fairest countries upon **the globe.** My sympathies became enlisted in behalf of these long-suffering and neglected people. Our country had conquered them and subjugated them to its own terms; and was there nothing more demanded for this bleeding, riven, **and** desolated country? Were there no hearts to commiserate the helpless condition of these perishing millions of souls **under the iron heel of papal power,** with all its soul-destroying **influences?** I could not avoid **the** impression that **an** important duty devolved upon Evangelical Christendom to try and do something for the moral elevation of this people, who had so long been "sitting in the region and shadow of death." Indeed, I felt that the honor **of** *American* Christianity most imperatively demanded that some effort should immediately **be** made. **So** strongly impressed was I of this that I wrote several articles for publication, hoping to enlist **an interest** among the churches and missionary boards; but my appeals met with **no** response, and I resolved, God helping **me, to** *go* *myself* to Mexico **and** do what **I** could **do** for **the** enlightenment **of** her long-neglected people. Although I could **not** *preach* the Gospel to them, **yet I felt that I** could, in ways adapted to my appropriate sphere, do something for bringing its blessings among them.

The unsettled condition of Mexico prevented me from going there immediately, yet I resolved to set my face thitherward, and wait the indications of God's Providence, in the confidence that an opportunity would be presented for the fulfillment of my cherished desires. In pursuance of this object, I closed my labors in Mississippi in May of 1847. It was with extreme reluctance that my patrons would accede to my plans of leaving them for going among the Mexicans, yet when they fully understood my motives, they finally acquiesced. However painful I found the breaking away from my long cherished friends, I realized I had a still greater trial before me, as I must go to Texas in order to get into Mexico, and I well knew that Texas, as well as Mexico, was not a place to which an unprotected woman would aspire to go, from any expectation of comfort or perhaps of safety. But I felt the word to be "Go forward;" and although the waves of uncertainty dashed high and loud, yet I must venture upon the simple command of God, believing that a promise was appended equal to the circumstances.

I girded on the armor of faith; took a final leave of the kindest of friends, and went to Vicksburg for taking a steamer down the Mississippi river. I took passage, without any definite conclusion which route I should take; whether I should go into Eastern Texas, by the way of Red River, or go to New Orleans, and there take a vessel for Western Texas. My *final* place of destination was fully decided, but the *way* of going to it, I must commit to Him who called me. I immediately went into my state-room, and sat down to contemplate my undertaking. All the absurdity of starting to Texas, with a view of going to Mexico, was permitted to take possession of me. How presumptuous it appeared to go to Texas, which, although then annexed to the United States, was, according to report, and general impression, peopled by outlaws and renegades from other lands. What would my parents and friends say if they knew of my mad purpose? On the other hand I reflected thus: Why have I taken this step? How came I possessed with the idea of going on such a hazardous expedition? Did it not come from above? Surely, the Lord has put this into my heart, or I never should have come to such a decision as starting for Mexico. He has inclined me to set my foot forward, and I will trust Him to be my guide and protector. My agitated and anxious feelings became calmed, and I arose, went out, and stood upon the guards of the steamer. While in peaceful contemplation, looking upon the beautiful scenery on the banks of the river, there came a little girl, about ten years of age, and stood beside me. I addressed her, as I usually do children with whom I fall in company while traveling, by ask-

3

ing her, "Where are you going?" In answer to my question she very readily replied, "I am going to Texas."

"Ah!" said I, "and I am going to Texas, too." Then I put the question, "To what part of Texas are you going?"

She replied, "I do not know, as I have never been there, but am going with my uncle to live with him." She added, "I will ask my uncle, and tell you to what place in Texas we are going."

I very soon went into the ladies saloon, and after having been seated some little time, there came in a very respectable appearing gentleman, who took a seat near, and addressed me, by saying, "My niece informs me you are going to Texas."

I replied that I was.

He inquired, "To what part of Texas are you going?"

Here was a dilemma, but I came up bravely to the occasion by replying, "I have no definite place of destination."

This elicited a more direct query, "But why, and for what purpose, do you go to Texas?"

I then gave him a brief detail of the motives which inspired me in turning my attention in that direction. But, as I doubted whether I would be able to carry out the design of immediately going among the Mexicans, I purposed to remain in Texas, for a time, and assist in the educational and religious interests of that new State.

The gentleman almost bounded from his seat, and with much evident pleasure congratulated me upon such a praiseworthy enterprise. He added, " We are truly in want of good teachers in Texas; indeed, it is the great and pressing need at this stage of progress in the State." He said, also, that before he left Texas for Washington, some three months previous, he was requested by the trustees of the Female Academy at Huntsville, Texas, to procure for them a lady teacher, but had failed to do so, as his time had been so completely occupied in business with the Government, concerning the establishment of mail routes in Texas, that he had not found time. " Besides," added he, " I could hardly venture to ask a well qualified young lady, with the unfavorable impressions which prevail against Texas, to go to the 'Lone Star State.' " He said he presumed the situation was still vacant, and proposed that I should go on in company with him and his niece and occupy it. He would regard it as a special favor if I would take charge of the little girl, and said he would gladly render me the necessary assistance for traveling in Texas, as I should find much difficulty for the lack of suitable conveyance.

I was inclined to believe that God, who had given me such cheerful confidence in his guiding hand, had provided this way for my entrance into Texas, and I was disposed to take this kind proposition into careful consideration, although made by an

entire stranger.   He was going by the way of the
Red River, and I should have nearly two days
travel before leaving the steamer, upon which I
had already taken passage, for further acquaintance. . At the close of the second day, I finally decided upon landing at the mouth of Red River,
and taking passage with my new-made friends.   I
found the little girl a pleasant young companion,
and the gentleman, in manners and conduct, such
as inspired my confidence.

The boat upon which we ascended the river was
quite small, as the depth of water would not admit
of the larger steamers.   The meandering course of
the stream made our trip slow and somewhat unpleasant, yet the consciousness that I was on the
way to the land to which the Lord had called me,
greatly lessened the tediousness.   When we arrived
opposite Alexandria, La., our craft ran upon a sand-
bar, and made a final stop.   All efforts to extricate
the boat seemed to be ineffectual, and for four days
we remained in the middle of the river, exposed to
the burning sun of June.   A more uncomfortable
condition could scarcely be imagined, and passengers and crew became quite disheartened.

CHAPTER IV.

THE river was daily becoming more shallow, and the hope of finding any other means of conveyance could not be indulged. Railroads, at that early day, especially in that region, were not found at every turn to convey waiting passengers to almost any point of compass. Neither, indeed, were stage coaches to be obtained in that portion of country in which our lot had cast us.

About the middle of the fourth day I began to feel somewhat as Bunyan's Pilgrim did in the cave of Giant Despair. His extremity was such as to remind him of a forgotten key which he carried in his bosom, by means of which he was enabled to unlock the strong gates of his prison, and he and his companion walked out of the dismal cell in which they were imprisoned, into light and liberty. The question arose in my mind, Are there no praying souls on board? God alone can help us, and I will make mention of the arm of Omnipotence, and see if there be any who will respond. I touched the key-note, and was rejoiced to find several of . the passengers who immediately caught the impulse. "God will be inquired of before deliverance comes," became the watchword. The afternoon was spent in rehearsing the dealings of God with us in times past, and in acknowledging our continued dependence upon Him. The means used were blest, as we believed in answer to prayer, and before sunset our boat was extricated from the cruel bar which so long had held us, and we were soon on our way again.

During our delay, my gentleman friend went to Alexandria, and there met one of the trustees of Huntsville Academy, who informed him they were still waiting for a teacher, and requested him to make a positive engagement with me to go directly on to Huntsville. We continued our way up the river as far as Natchitoches, La., where we landed, for going to Texas. A carriage and horses were purchased, and we traveled the remainder of the way, which was three hundred miles, by land. The miserable and desolate looking country which I had pictured, in my imagination, Texas to be, became transformed into one of the most beautiful regions I had ever before beheld. The splendid trees, the verdant plains, and great variety of wild flowers, conspired to make the scene an enchanting one. Instead of a wild and uncultivated population, I found many highly refined and intelligent people, who had but a short time previous emigrated from the Southern States to Texas. At Nacogdoches, a place of considerable importance, I was most urgently requested to remain as teacher for several families. The gentleman said, "**If you are not** pleased with Huntsville, **write us, and** we will send a carriage **and bring** you back." But I *was* pleased **with** Huntsville. I found a town of some five or six hundred inhabitants, most of whom had come to Texas after the annexation to the United States. Several of the families had daughters, who had been partially educated before they emigrated, and they greatly desired the **con**tinuance of their education in their adopted **home. My** reception was most **cordial, and as one after** another welcomed me with **the warmest** greetings, **I** said to myself, surely " **My** lines are fallen in pleasant places." **Was it** singular that I sometimes cast my mind back to the time of my starting for Texas; when, in my lonely stateroom, on the Mississippi steamer, I indulged in painful and doubtful soliloquy upon the adventure **I** was about making? After realizing such wonderful displays of **the lov**ing kindness of my Heavenly Father **in my be**half, could I ever doubt again in following wherever **He, in His** Providence, may see fit to **lead me? No, *never;*** but **we** shall see. There are other **steeps to** climb before life's work is finished, and faith **may again** falter—but we will not anticipate. " Sufficient unto the day is the evil thereof."

I commenced my labors at Huntsville under the

most favorable auspices, and various departments
of usefulness opened before me. Besides week-day
and Sunday-schools, I lent a helping hand in writing for some religious and educational periodicals,
which were then just in their incipiency. As I
could not venture among the Mexicans at that
time, I felt that my duty lay, for the time being,
among the Texans. Every thing conspired to
make my situation peculiarly delightful, and I
worked with a purpose commensurate with the demands. Surely, I thought, I am sailing on beautiful waters. But, oh! when one year rolled
around my overtaxed system gave way, and I was
reluctantly obliged to succumb. How keenly I
felt the blow! To give up my dearly cherished
work was, in my estimation, an unparalleled mis-
fortune. My nervous system was much affected,
and my mind indulged in very uncomfortable
vagaries. An unfulfilled responsibility seemed
resting upon me, and my constant grief was I must
die and leave the anticipated work of my life un-
done. On one hand was a life purpose unaccom-
plished, and on the other a sinking, dying body.
I was much relieved one day by words of comfort
from a cherished Christian friend. Making my
doleful lamentations to him, he replied, with much
emphasis, "You are not called to die yet, but you
will live to accomplish some work for God." I
replied, Oh! can such a boon be granted me, I will
welcome life on any shore, and among any people,

however inhospitable! After several months of intense suffering, both of body and of mind, a new lease of life was granted, by a partial restoration of my health, so I was able again to resume my labors.

My bitter experience had taught me to take better care of the tenement in which I dwelt, and I endeavored to limit my duties to the amount of physical ability I possessed. I assisted in the establishment of schools, devoting a portion of my time to writing for publication. A little book, entitled "*Texas*, 1850," was the product of my pen, in which I endeavored to show the great need of evangelical laborers in Texas, not only on its own account, but on account of its prospective influence over Mexico. I do not think I made a very striking exhibition of authorship, but the desire of benefiting those neglected countries by representing their real condition, and their pressing wants, perhaps afforded an excuse for the attempt. I remained two years longer, building up schools in different parts of the State, and ever and anon casting my eye towards the dark regions beyond, with earnest longings for the time when I would be permitted to carry the torch of Divine Truth to the millions of souls in Mexico who were buried beneath the rubbish of papal error and superstition.

CHAPTER V.

Entrance upon **work** for the Mexican people—Important information **gained** through Rev. Daniel Baker—Decide to go to Brownsville—A Mexican population there—Sight of a *live* Mexican—Heartfelt sympathy for **the** whole nation —**No place for** boarding could be obtained—Home of my **own—Could not go into** Mexico with the Bible—The laws **prohibiting Protestant Christianity—Opened a school for Mexican** children on the **American side of** the Rio Grande—Encouraged **in** my **efforts in** teaching the Bible —The parents making no objections, **but** desiring the Bible themselves—Dangers of living on the frontier—Trust in Providence—Exchanging a Bible for a "saint"—Distribution of Bibles among Mexicans on the American and Mexican side of the river.

IN the spring of 1852 I believed the time had fully come for me to commence my work for the Mexican people. I had gained some very important information in regard to my probable success, through Rev. Daniel Baker, D.D., a Presbyterian minister, who, in 1850, had ascended the Rio Grande River as far as Roma, a distance of two hundred miles, for investigating the condition of the country for evangelical work. He represented the Mexicans as accessible, and many of them manifesting the desire for instruction in the Bible.

I left Jefferson, Eastern Texas, in May, and went to New Orleans to take passage on a vessel for

Brazos Santiago, near the mouth of the Rio
Grande River. I purposed going to Brownsville,
a place situated about sixty miles up the river,
opposite Matamoras, Mexico. The steamship for
which I waited brought news of the invasion of
Brownsville, by Indians, of a very alarming character. This condition of affairs, prevailing at the
place of my destination, presented somewhat of an
obstacle in the way of the further prosecution of
my journey, as I had hoped that things had become
sufficiently settled on the frontier to insure personal safety at least. But could I turn back because of difficulties in the way? I thought of the
trials of "Pilgrim," who met lions in the way,
and also of the advice given him "To keep in the
middle of the road, and the lions could not harm
him." "Duty to God" was my watchword, and
on His powerful arm I trusted for protection, and I
resolved to go forward. Remaining in New Orleans over the Sabbath, I attended what was then
Rev. Dr. Scott's church, where I heard a sermon
from a stranger (Dr. S. being absent) which fully
established my faith in God's Providential dealings
with his people. Although that stranger, who was
a foreigner, judging by his dialect, may never
know, in this world, the comforting message he
brought to me on that occasion, perhaps a future
day will reveal that it was a word spoken in
season to one soul at least. With renewed courage
I took passage, and crossed the Gulf of Mexico,

landing at Brazos, and passing over an arm of the
sea, arrived at Point Isabel. There I took a stage
for Brownsville.

A new sensation seized me when I saw, for the
first time, a *Mexican,* a representative of the nation
for which I had entertained such profound interest.
I did not feel, as many others have expressed, that
the *sight* of a Mexican was enough to disgust one
with the whole nation. A heartfelt sympathy was
revived, not by the prepossessing exterior, surely,
but because a priceless soul was incased in it for whom
the Savior had died. And a whole nation of souls,
shut out from the light of the gospel of salvation,
pressed with an increased influence upon my heart.
Although I was coming into a land of new and
untried scenes, yet I felt God's presence encompassing me, and I repeated the lines of Madame
Guyon,

> "To me belongs nor time nor space,
> My country is in every place;
> I can be calm and free from care,
> On any shore, *since God is there.*"

Just before arriving in Brownsville, the driver
of the stage asked me where I wished to be left.
I replied, "Take me to the best hotel in town."
He answered, "There is no hotel in Brownsville."
This intelligence was somewhat of a damper upon
my feelings and prospects, and I mused upon the
unpleasant condition of a stranger arriving in such
a place after nine o'clock at night. After a little

time the driver said, "I know a German woman who sometimes takes lady boarders, and I will take you to her house." Accordingly, I was set down at this woman's door, and I found my way inside, and asked for a night's lodging. The woman kindly received me, and I passed the night very comfortably.

At ten o'clock the next day I sallied out in quest of more commodious quarters. I found an American family, with which I was invited to remain a few days, but they could not give me permanent board. After several applications for a boarding-place, I was finally compelled to provide a home for myself, which I did, by renting two rooms, one for a residence, and the other I intended appropriating to school purposes. The day before opening my school, I went to my rooms, but not under very auspicious circumstances. At dark, I had no bed to sleep on, nor did I know how I was to obtain my breakfast, to say nothing of a supper. But before the hour of retiring came, a Mexican woman brought me a cot, an American woman sent me a pillow, and a German woman came and said she would cook my meals and bring them to me. Did I not feel rich that night as I retired to my humble cot? Indeed, I never closed my eyes in sleep with more profound feelings of thankfulness to God. I fully believed I was where my Divine Master had called me to go—upon the border of that land where I had so long desired to be—and to whose people I trusted the Lord would make me eminently useful.

Next morning I opened my school with five pupils, but more promised. The education of the children seemed the most feasable means of benefitting the people at that time, and I opened a school although upon the American side of the Rio Grande. The laws of Mexico, at that time, most positively forbade the introduction of Protestant Christianity in any form, and had I gone into Mexico proper for the purpose of teaching the Bible, I should have been imprisoned.

That portion of Texas between the Rio Grande and Nueces Rivers had been claimed by Mexico previous to the late war, but the United States had conquered, and, consequently, it was under our government. Some thousands of Mexican people preferred remaining in their old homes, which fact gave me an opportunity of laboring among Mexicans under the protection of our own government. I was truly happy in a short time in obtaining some thirty or forty Mexican children, and giving them daily instruction in the Bible, against which the parents manifested no objection. I found some who could read in the Spanish language, and a few who had acquired some knowledge of the English. The parents were greatly desirous their children should learn the English language, and become Americanized, and hence my school received popular favor on that account. To be able to put the

Bible into the hands of three or four dozen Mexican children, and give them instruction in its blessed teachings, I felt to be an unspeakable privilege. Although the work might look **small to the eye** of human reason, yet faith bade **me hope it** might prove a *beginning*, and I was satisfied to work **on, even in** this small way. The parables of our Savior afforded me much encouragement, especially those in which He compares the kingdom of heaven **to** a grain of mustard seed, which, when sown, is the least of all seeds, yet from it sprang a **tree** sufficiently large for the fowls of heaven **to lodge** in its branches; also "to leaven, **which a woman** took (there was a **good deal of significance in the** fact that it was a *woman*) and hid **in three measures** of meal, until the **whole was** leavened."

My exposed situation made me exceedingly timid, especially by night, as Indians were reported to be upon the outskirts of the town, and liable any night to break in and commit depredations. Besides, there were any number of lawless Mexicans prowling about for purposes of theft, etc. I was told "there were plenty who would take my life for the dress I took off at night." My dwelling was near a house in which resided Caravajal, a Mexican general, who had besieged Matamoras a few months before, and who was liable to an arrest any time by the authorities of Matamoras. **In** order to repel an attack, **he** kept a body-guard stationed around his house at night. Knowing I was alone, and unprotected, he kindly informed me that his guard would afford ample protection to my premises also; but I did not feel my safety augmented by having Caravajal, with all his dangers, so near me, even though he had provided himself the means of repelling his enemies. In case of an attack, my domicil, with its slender walls, would as likely be penetrated by bullets as his. During the first month of my residence in Brownsville, I suffered much anxiety, and kept almost a constant watch all through the lonely hours of night. Finally, I came to the conclusion that, should my house be disturbed by any of those marauders, I should feel it my duty to leave the field of labor, however inviting, in other respects, it might be. But after watching some weeks, and no visible disturbance occurring, I resolved to remain, continue my work, and trust in Providence. I was enabled to relinquish all my fears, and slept quietly, with a feeling of security as much as if I knew a sentinel was placed at each corner of my dwelling. "The name of the Lord *is* a strong tower; the righteous runneth into it, and is safe." My school prospered, and I was encouraged in finding the Mexican children susceptible of moral and mental improvement. Many of them I found addicted to the vices peculiar to their race; but, by proper instruction, I soon observed a very decided change. I was told by an American gentleman, who had had considerable acquaintance with Mexican character, that stealing was inherent among those people, and could not be eradicated. My experience entirely disproved this assertion, as after a few months, children, who would take things which did not belong to them, became convinced of the error, and entirely abandoned the practice. I endeavored to impress them that the Bible was God's Book, and what He taught us in that we must obey. The instruction given to the children was conveyed by them to the parents, and they, too, wished to see the Book from whence the instruction was derived. A mother of one of the little girls of my school came to my door one day, bringing her " saint," as she called it; she said she had prayed to it all her life, and it had never done her any good, and asked me if I would take the " saint " and give her a Bible for it. I very readily made the exchange. Indeed, I was well enough pleased to give her *two* Bibles, as she said she had a friend over in Matamoras who wanted the good Book also.*

I visited many of the homes of my pupils, and wherever I could find any of the family who could read, I left a Bible, or a portion of it. I was much gratified in finding many of the adults who could read in their own language. This fact greatly enlarged my prospect of benefiting the Mexican people, as they almost uniformly manifested a great desire to see what had been a proscribed Book to

---

* This woman and her daughter afterward became my most efficient helpers in the distribution of the Bible in Mexico.

4

them. I believed the Bible to be the main instrumentality of renovating that long-neglected race, and I aimed to extend its circulation among all whom I could by any means reach. But there were the millions upon the other side of the Rio Grande, who, by the most stringent laws of the government, were shut up in impenetrable darkness. When I cast my eye over into that priest-bound country, my heart yearned for its emancipation from the dreadful tyranny of papal laws. But upon my distressing thoughts a light suddenly arose by ascertaining that Bibles were being carried over into that dark land by the Mexicans on the American side of the river. Although I knew the transfer of Bibles into Mexico to be a direct violation of the laws of the country, yet I felt no conscientious scruples in lending them my aid; for I felt God's Word to be above all human law, and no earthly power had the right of withholding it from any of God's accountable creatures.

Dozens of Bibles were carried over the river, and distributed among the people, who gladly received them. I became convinced that good might be done, even by this slight skirmishing upon the outskirts of the enemy's camp. The missils which were being sent were of a character to do powerful execution; and I doubted not but it would ultimately be seen that, by them, essential damage had been received in this kingdom of darkness, where Satan had so long reigned with undisputed sway.

CHAPTER VI.

Recruits of the enemy from **abroad—Looking to** God for help against the mighty—A French convent proposed—Resolved to erect a Protestant seminary by its side—Started **for** New Orleans—Perils by sea—Proposed seminary regarded chimerical by the ministers of New Orleans—Could not abandon my purpose—Protestant Christians must aid me in building a seminary—Soliciting funds—Encounters with two business men—Aid from **the Presbyterian** Board of Education.

IN the midst of the most sanguine expectations of permanent good upon this **frontier, I** was surprised, one day, **by hearing that** several priests and nuns had come **from** France to establish their head-quarters at Brownsville. They had brought means for erecting a convent, for the evident purpose of educating the youth of the Rio Grande Valley. Suddenly and unexpectedly, all my prospects of usefulness there seemed completely **frustrated**; for **what** could I do, with **such** an array of influences against Protestantism and the Bible? But, could I abandon the field, and leave **it** in the hands of foreign priests and nuns? Indeed, I could not get my own consent to run before popery, while I held in my hand **such a** powerful spiritual weapon as the Word of God, and I was enabled to **carry the** matter to the throne of grace, and wait for **Divine** direction. **I spent** whole nights in

prayer to God. During one of those seasons in
which I was earnestly seeking for guidance, a light
suddenly dawned on my mind, from these words in
the book of Revelation: "These shall make war
with the Lamb, and the Lamb shall overcome
them: for he is Lord of lords, and King of kings:
and they that are with Him are called, and chosen,
and faithful." The impression that these words
made upon my heart, immediately settled the question of my remaining. Although single-handed
and alone, yet, with the assurance derived from
these words of Scripture, I felt stronger than my
enemies; and I resolved to stay and maintain my
post. In order to make a successful stand, I must
have a building which would bear some comparison with the party with which I had to compete.
My accommodations hitherto had been exceedingly
limited; and, as I could obtain no aid from the inhabitants of that region, I resolved to go to the
United States and secure the means for building a
Protestant seminary at Brownsville. If France
could afford to send four millions of dollars to the
United States for educational purposes, (as she did
that year) I felt that the Protestant Christians of
the United States could afford a few hundred for
the Rio Grande; so, I closed my school, and set my
face toward my native land, feeling quite assured of
prompt and efficient aid. The scene of my departure was calculated to deepen my interest for these
people. As I was about starting on the stage for

Brazos, I was surrounded by the Mexican girls and their mothers, each uttering the earnest request, "come back," "*come back very soon*," and they stood and watched me with tearful eyes, until I passed out of their sight. When I arrived at Brazos, I could find no conveyance to New Orleans but a schooner, and that very small and inconvenient. It being the time of the year for violent "Northers," we had a most tempestuous and dangerous passage. We were twelve days out, and for some four or five, we lay to in the middle of the Gulf, surging amid the angry waves. Great fears were entertained that our puny bark would go to the bottom of the sea; and for several nights I did not get into my berth, as the violent rocking of the vessel made it impossible to obtain a moment's rest. Often did my natural timidity get the ascendency, and I would say to myself, "If I ever set my foot on land again, I will never more attempt to cross the Gulf of Mexico." But I was tried in this fearful manner, until I was brought to exclaim, "As long as my Heavenly Father wills, will I trust my life at his bidding, and, should He see fit to take me hence in this manner, I would say, 'Even so, come Lord Jesus.'" We finally arrived in New Orleans, and learned that our vessel had been published in the *Daily Picayune*, "Supposed to be lost at sea." With gratitude for God's preserving care, I hastened with my darling object to see my Protestant friends, who, I felt

quite assured would realize its importance and
feasibility as I did.   But my first presentation met
with a decided disapproval.   The idea of establishing a Protestant institution upon that papal frontier
was regarded as chimerical and absurd in the extreme.   The counselors to whom I resorted were
some of the wisest and most reliable clergymen of
the South, and, how could I lightly regard the
judgment and advice of these Christian men?   Yet,
how was I to dispose of the impression that God
had put the work into my hands, and required me
to prosecute it.   In inclining to follow the advice
of my friends, the denunciations passed upon some
in olden time would meet me, " Woe unto the rebellious children, saith the Lord, who take counsel,
but not of *Me*."   I could no more throw off my
duty to God in this matter, than I could throw off
my existence; and I resolved to go forward, and if
needs be, take the kingdom of heaven by violence,
in obedience to my rightful Lord and Master.   A
Protestant seminory *must* be reared in the Rio
Grande Valley, under the auspices of Protestant
Christians of the United States.

I remained in New Orleans a month; and, by
persevering in the presentation of my cause, in all its
various bearings and necessities, my most strenuous
opposers became my warmest friends.   The important
query was raised, whether I had sufficient fortitude
to withstand the difficulties which I must necessarily encounter in obtaining funds, as well as in

sustaining a Protestant institution in the midst of so many opposing influences. I called, one day, upon a Christian gentleman, who most kindly admonished me that the undertaking was entirely incompatible with the character of a lady, and advised me not to expose myself in collecting funds in the manner I was pursuing. He said, "You will receive rebuffs and insults which will kill all the finer instincts of the soul." I felt there was much truth in what he said; and, thanking him for his candid expressions, I left his house with the feeling that I never would enter a business house again with my object. But another house was but a few steps, which I had been informed was the office of a good man, and an impulse seized me, to go in, and see what he had to say to me. Accordingly, I stepped in, and saw several gentlemen sitting at their desks, but I did not know the one to whom I wished to speak. I hastily cast my eye around, and selected the one who, I thought, possessed the most benevolent countenance, and approached him. He very politely requested me to be seated. I introduced myself by presenting my credentials, which I had received from the ministers of New Orleans, and commenced making apologies that a woman should be engaged in such an unlady-like enterprize.

"By no means," said he, "is it contrary to the most refined delicacy of the female sex to be engaged in works of philanthropy for the elevation

of fallen humanity. It is woman's proper calling.
The Savior forever sanctified the services of women
by the commendation he gave to them. Do not
hesitate to go forward in any work of benevolence
to which your Master may call you." Were not
the timely words of this man like heavenly balm to
my lacerated heart? It seemed Jesus spoke, and
said to me, "Fear not, it is your Father's good
pleasure, to give you the kingdom;" and I went
forward, determined never to falter again. Although I did not get much money in New Orleans,
yet, I obtained letters of recommendation from
several of the most influential men in the city.

Leaving New Orleans, I went to Louisville, Ky.,
and was kindly received; but, as the churches were
engaged in making their annual contributions to
other objects, I received no present aid, but was
promised that at some future time they would assist
me in my enterprise. I then went on to Philadelphia, arriving the 4th day of March, 1853, at 2
o'clock in the morning. At 9 o'clock of the same
morning I was wending my way to the rooms of
the Presbyterian Board of Education, with a letter
of introduction from Rev. Dr. Hill, of Louisville,
to the secretaries, Drs. Chester and Van Rensselaer.
With these reverend gentlemen I had to pass another severe and trying ordeal. All the difficulties
of the enterprise were again brought forward, and
paraded with considerable embellishment. I met
them with arguments, which I thought ought to

have weight, but they seemed to make but little impression upon either of the gentlemen, particularly upon Dr. Chester. He seemed determined that my enterprise *should* prove a failure. After talking some time, without making any apparent impression favorable to the cause, I arose and said, "Gentlemen, I leave the responsibilities of the proper education of the youth of that portion of country upon your hands. I have done what I can, and henceforth my skirts are clear of the criminal negligence of leaving the beloved youth of the Rio Grande Valley to the baleful influence of foreign popery." Dr. Chester immediately arose to his feet, and with much emphasis, said, "I am not going to take the Rio Grande upon my shoulders, *you* are the one to bear that burden. We have fully tested your proper understanding of the difficult enterprise, and your ability in carrying it forward. We are now ready to inquire of your wants." I replied, "I must have *money*." "How much," said he, "do you want of *us?*" I felt quite subdued and modestly replied, "two or three hundred dollars." He replied, "You must not leave Philadelphia with less than *five* hundred. If the Board of Education do not see proper to give you two hundred, Dr. Van Rensselaer and I will pay it out of our own pockets, and the remaining three hundred I will put you in the way of obtaining from the Presbyterian churches of the city."

5

I remained a month and obtained the amount promised, and then went on to Boston, and obtained from the churches of that city another five hundred. I became fully confident that a Protestant seminary would surely rear its head by the side of the French convent which was already rising upon the distant Rio Grande. Oh! how my heart exulted in the prospect of the Bible having its place and exerting its due influence upon the hearts and minds of the rising generation of that land!

CHAPTER VII.

Laborious work to obtain money for the Mexicans—Some
proposed bullets instead of Bibles—Variety of treatment
—Helped by a Catholic—Treated rudely by a lady—Not
discouraged—Find many friends to the cause—Many
liberal donations—Finally obtain sufficient funds for my
seminary building.

THE fatigue attending my arduous duties, compelled me to suspend my labors for a portion of
the summer months. Early in the autumn, I started
from Pittsburg, Pa., by steamer, intending to take
the entire course of the Ohio and Mississippi rivers,
stopping at all towns and cities where I had any
prospect of obtaining money. The prejudices existing against the Mexicans, engendered during the
late war, often proved great barriers to my success.
The sentiment was expressed by many, that "the
Mexicans were a people just fit to be exterminated
from the earth." Even ministers of the gospel
said to me, "We had better send bullets and gun-
powder to Mexico than Bibles." Of such I generally asked the question, "What class of persons did
our Savior come from heaven to save, the righteous or the wicked?" Just such a class of sinners
as the Mexicans. Sometimes I would receive donations in this way, "We do not care for the Mexicans, but, seeing you so devoted to their cause, we

will give something for *your* sake." One man, after applying all the contemptible epithets to the Mexicans he could think of, said, "Out of pity to you, whose appearance and spirit I like, in having such a bad cause in hand, I will give you ten dollars for your own personal use." I declined receiving it for myself, saying, "*Money* can not compensate me for what I am doing, but, if you will give it me to appropriate as I wish, I will do it upon my own responsibility." He consented, but I could not set him down as a "cheerful giver." At some places where I stopped, if I could obtain ten dollars a day, I would remain ten days, until I would get one hundred. At some cities, such as Cincinnati and Louisville, I received very liberal aid. Pursuing my arduous way, "through rude and stormy scenes," I arrived in Natchez, Miss., in March, 1854. Here I found a wealthy and benevolent people, and I made rapid strides toward the completion of my enterprise. The wealthy class of people lived mostly in the country, on plantations, and my canvassing was generally some distance from the city. Occasionally, friends would give me a ride, but usually I walked, and frequently I traveled some eight or ten miles a day; but my labor was so generously rewarded, I forgot the fatigue of the way. One day, I went to see a lady who was recommended as being very benevolent. Upon inquiry, I was told the lady was absent, but that her husband was at home, and I could see him if I wished.   I was ushered into his room, and, after respectful salutation, said, "I came to see your wife."

He very pleasantly replied that perhaps he would do as well, and, if I pleased, I might deliver my message to him.   Thus encouraged, I gave a very elaborate delineation of the great need of evangelical laborers in that papal land, and especially as it was becoming overrun by foreign Roman Catholicism.   I was unusually eloquent upon the subject, as my listener manifested such a deep interest.

When I concluded, he arose, went to his desk, took out twenty dollars, and handed me, saying, "I presume you do not know that I am a Roman Catholic."

There were a few "feathers dropped out of my cap," at that moment, and the most profound mortification took possession of me.   But his smiling face re-assured me, and I very meekly said I *did not* know he was a Catholic.

He replied, "I am so by name only.   My parents and all my ancestors were Roman Catholics, but I have no preferences for that religion. My wife is an Episcopalian, and I attend her church.   He continued, "I am convinced you will do good to those people, and I have very cheerfully contributed my aid."

We parted the best of friends, and I told him that in future I would take a better lookout, lest I might find more dangerous soundings than I had found with him.

My pleasant experience in Natchez will perhaps warrant the recital of one little episode, showing some of the more trying vicissitudes to which solicitors of money may be subjected.

I was, while in Natchez, directed to call upon a very wealthy lady. She was a member of the Presbyterian Church, and although somewhat peculiar, it was thought that the proper presentation of my cause might elicit a liberal donation. I called, and was taken into her presence by the servant. I introduced myself in my usual way, and presented the object of my visit with becoming propriety; but it seemed she was in a most ungracious mood, for she replied with great vehemence, "I have nothing to give you, besides I know nothing about you. You may be an impostor, as there are many going about under like pretences."

I was stung to the quick by her unjust allusion, and hastened to produce my papers, some of which were recommendations from members of her own church. I said, "I do not care for your money, but I do wish to convince you that I am not an impostor." But she paid no heed to what I said, and with most angry demonstrations ordered her servant to open the door, and bade me go out. I walked out, of course, but with the deepest humiliation I ever experienced in my life.

With flushed face, and falling tears, I went on my way until I came to another stately mansion to which I was also directed. I hesitated entering, as from my recent experience I would gladly have avoided exposing myself again to heartless and bitter cruelty. But, I reflected, benevolence and humanity are not perished from the earth because of the conduct of this woman; her spirit is the exception, not the rule. I entered, although with a trembling heart; but upon my first introduction I saw I had a different person with whom to deal, from the one I had just encountered. The lady of the house received me with the utmost kindness, made me a liberal donation, and when I left accompanied me to her gate, and pointed to the house I had just left, saying, "There lives my sister, go there. I know she will give you something for your cause." I did not tell her I had already been there. I would not wound her feelings by the recital of her sister's conduct toward me.

Some two or three years after, I was traveling on business connected with my work, and stopped in one of the Northern cities, where I was informed of a shocking railroad accident which had just occurred near by. A lady who had visited the scene of the disaster, told me of one of the sufferers, a lady from Natchez, Miss. By the description, I was confident it was the person from whom I had received such ungracious treatment. The poor woman, with broken limbs and lacerated flesh, was bewailing her great affliction, and the painful deprivation of the comforts of her palatial home in

Mississippi.   A little shanty, from which she could not be removed, was all she could have for her accommodation.   My heart was moved at the recital of her distresses, and could I possibly have gone to her, would most gladly have tried to minister to her comfort.   I could only put up the prayer that God would comfort her, and forgive her for so misjudging me.   But I soon passed on, and never heard of her more.

CHAPTER VIII.

Return to Brownsville—Fourteen months away—The convent
built—Contracted with a responsible man for the erection
of my building—Rented rooms, and opened my school
again—School soon full—Commenced Bible and Tract
distribution—Unbelief of Protestants—Great trials on
that account—In 1854 enter my new seminary—Dedica-
tion—Much encouragement by new openings of usefulness.

BUT I have wandered from my narrative, and I
will return to my journey toward the land of
my adoption.   From Natchez I went to New Orleans, and took passage on a vessel for Brazos.   I
had been absent from Brownsville fourteen months,
and I began to feel quite solicitous to know how
matters stood in my destined field of labor.

When I arrived in Brownsville, I found the
convent completed—a spacious three story building, situated in the most conspicuous part of the
town, and in it were gathered most of the girls of
the Rio Grande.   Nothing daunted, I contracted
with a responsible man for the erection of my Seminary building; rented my former rooms, and
opened my school again.   The attendance was
small at first, but before the close of the second
month all my former pupils had returned, and several new ones came, also.   I possessed one important advantage, namely, the Mexicans desired their

children to learn the English, and as that language
was but imperfectly taught in the convent, many
left and came to me on that account. My school
prospered beyond my most sanguine expectations.
I renewed my Bible and Tract distribution, and
found an increasing interest for the Word of Life,
both on the Texan and Mexican side of the Rio
Grande.

Here let me state one painful trial I had to encounter. The bitterest thing with which I had to
contend was the incredulity which prevailed among
the American population as to any good being done
to the Mexican people. Some professed Protestant
Christians were among the number; and, indeed, I
regret to say, my greatest opposers were among
those who believed they had been recipients of the
blessings of the Gospel of Christ.

"What can we do for such a hopeless race?" was
the usual suggestion when I attempted to urge the
importance of evangelical labor in behalf of the
Mexicans. My reply uniformly was, "Give them
the Gospel, which is the antidote for all moral
evils. The extreme degradation in which we find
them is for the want of the ameliorating influence
of Bible Christianity." Some went so far as to
say, "The Mexicans have a religion good enough
for them, and we had better let them alone." My
zeal and efforts were regarded as a sort of insanity,
and I more dreaded meeting a Protestant Christian
in my rounds of Bible distribution than I did a

Romish **priest.** From the latter **I** expected persecution, but from the former I had reason **to look**
for sympathy for Christ's sake. Sometimes **I** almost staggered under the misconstructions put **up-**
on missionary **labors for** the **poor** despised **Mexi-**
cans.

One Sabbath afternoon I was sitting in my room,
musing upon **the** probabilities of any successful results of **my** efforts, **and** came quite near falling into the incredulous views of my Protestant friends.
My reflections were, " Why should I presume to be
so much wiser than those who have had much more
acquaintance with Mexican character than I have
had ? Surely, **I** thought, **I am quite too** independent in my views, and I will suspend my wild operations." Arriving **at** this stage of my soliloquies,
over and above came a voice, although not heard
by mortal ears, yet equally as impressive : " Go ye
into all the world and preach the gospel to every
creature." " *Every creature ?*" said **I** : " **does not**
this command embrace the Mexicans ? Surely **it**
does ; and it is Christ who gives this **command,**
and I will obey Him although I offend all else."
I arose immediately, determined to do my duty ;
and although all the Mexicans should come up on
the left hand in the great day, as **my** Protestant
friends seemed to have doomed them to do, it shall
be said of **me,** " She has done what she could " **for**
their salvation. I took some books and **went out**
again administering **the** Word of Life, and was ev-

ery-where thankfully received. "*Muchas gracias*" (many thanks) were uniformly expressed as I passed into their hands some portion of the Scriptures. I felt I was sowing seed which God had commanded to be sown " beside all waters," and I was determined to persevere, believing that " His word would not return void, but would accomplish that which He pleased, and prosper in the thing whereunto He sent it."

I found opportunities of sending hundreds of Bibles and hundreds of thousands of pages of the Tract Society's publications, in Spanish, into Mexico; and although the living teacher could not accompany them, yet I had faith to believe that the same Spirit which indited the Word could enlighten the spiritual sense of these people into the knowledge of those truths whereby their souls might be delivered from the bondage of sin and Satan, although shut up in the prison-house of papal power.

In the autumn of 1854 I entered my new seminary. This was an auspicious event. The days of labor and scenes of anxious solicitude were all forgotten on the morning I assembled my pupils for the first time in this Protestant institution. I explained to them that the building had been given by Christian friends abroad for their benefit, and endeavored to impress them with the vast importance of improving the privileges it would afford them to the best advantage possible. With my Mexican girls, I consecrated this new edifice to God by reading a portion of Scripture and by prayer. The American Bible and Tract Societies of New York continued to supply my demands for books; although I often wondered at their liberality, considering the very unpopular work I had in hand. I used often to think, in reference to the indifference which prevailed so extensively towards Mexico and her people, that the Lord had chosen me for the work because I was so very insignificant, and it mattered little if I did spend my poor life and services among the Mexicans. Sometimes I would take a view of the stupendous character of the undertaking — the *beginning* of a work upon a nation comprising eight millions of immortal souls! I would wonder why the Lord did not select a more efficient agent—some minister of the Gospel whose capacity was adequate to the great demand. Then would come up before me the declaration of the Apostle: "Has not God chosen the *weak* things of this world to confound the things which are mighty, that no flesh should glory in his presence?" I had to acknowledge that it was God's own economy to select just such a weak instrument as myself. His Word, which was my principal instrumentality, was just as powerful in my weak hands as in those of a learned doctor of divinity. When discouragements arose from not seeing the immediate results of my labors, a voice would seem to say to me, "What is that to thee? follow thou me." I was made willing to labor all my life, upon the simple command and promise of God, even though I might never witness any visible results, in the belief that a harvest would be gathered, although it might not be until I lay in my grave.

CHAPTER IX.

Need of help—The appeal made—The case stated—Letter
published by the American and Foreign Christian Union
—An effort made to find a suitable colporteur—None
could be found—Become a colporteur myself—The A. &
F. C. U. furnishing an assistant in my school—Incidents
of Bible work—Murder of a German Protestant.

IN 1855 I felt the need of assistance, and I ventured to write a letter to Rev. Dr. Kirk, of Boston, Mass., asking for a colporteur for the Mexican
frontier. The letter, quite unexpectedly to me, was
published in the magazine of the American and Foreign Christian Union for August, 1855. I will copy
the letter, and also the remarks of the editor. It
was headed—

"A VOICE FROM THE RIO GRANDE.

"The following letter from Miss Rankin, one of
the worthy daughters of New England, who, by
much sacrifice and indomitable perseverance, has
succeeded in establishing a seminary for Mexican
young ladies, in Brownsville, on the Texas side of
the Rio Grande, which separates the United States
from Mexico, will be read with much interest.

"It was addressed to one of the Board of Directors (a personal friend) with the view to obtain a lay
missionary for that important, yet neglected field

which she has so generously and praiseworthily entered, and which, under the Divine blessing, she is cultivating, with the prospect of the most encouraging results. It was not designed for publication. We trust, however, that the writer will pardon us for submitting it to our readers, whose sympathies and prayers and charities we desire to elicit in behalf of the people with whom she has chosen to take her abode.

"It is proper to add that the Board are now engaged in efforts to procure a suitable laborer to send into that field. But one laborer there is not enough. In that great valley and along the Mexican border there should be many missionaries employed, and to those to whom God has intrusted the means for their support they must appeal for the funds necessary to sustain them. We have done but little—alas! much too little—for that interesting portion of our own nation, and we hope that the facts contained in the subjoined letter will lead to liberal contributions for its benefit. But to the letter:

"BROWNSVILLE, *April,* 1855.

"REV. DR. KIRK:

"*Dear Sir*—Convinced that you have a sympathy with whatever appertains to the interest of Christ's kingdom, I take the liberty of calling your attention to this remote land, where, and on the border of which, are thousands of immortal souls under the influence of Popery, in its most enslaving and debasing forms. You are fully acquainted with Romanism, and, therefore, I need not describe to you the character of this soul-destroying agency of the arch-enemy Satan. I presume also, that I need not describe the painful emotions awakened in the heart by daily witnessing the sad influence of that system, so wisely calculated to lead immortal souls to endless ruin.

"We have in Brownsville some three or four thousand Mexicans, who have escaped the dreaded influence of a corrupt priesthood of their own country, in whose moral condition and wants my sympathies are deeply enlisted, and in whose behalf I now write. The enterprise in which I was engaged when last in your city I have, with the blessing of God, carried out successfully. A Protestant seminary is reared in front of papal Mexico, and within its walls are gathered Mexican girls, whose improvement encourages me to hope that their consciences may become enlightened, and that they will embrace the Gospel, which can save their souls. I trust it may ultimately be seen that this institution is one of the instrumentalities by which God intends to disenthrall benighted Mexico from the dominion of popery.

"The object to which I wish more particularly to draw your attention is the importance of having a colporteur here to circulate Bibles and other religious publications among the Mexicans generally. To convince you of the importance of this, I will mention some facts in my own experience. Although I felt my calling to be the instruction of children and youth, yet in my efforts to benefit them my spirit could have no rest without making an attempt to do something to enlighten the adults. I had but little faith in regard to my success, as the Mexicans appeared so completely enveloped in the darkness of superstition, and had six Jesuit priests

to guard their ignorance.   But I resolved upon
making the attempt ; and accordingly sent to the
American Bible and Tract Societies, and procured
books in the Spanish language, and commenced the
distribution in the face of the priests, whom I met
at almost every corner.   In almost every instance
the books were thankfully received, and in many
cases I ascertained that they were faithfully read.
About two months ago I received another box of
Bibles and Tracts from New York.   I called in a
Mexican man to open the box, and explained to
him the object of their being sent here, gave him a
Bible, and told him he might speak to his country-
men about them.   He returned next day and said
a Mexican lady had been reading his Bible, that
she believed it to be the truth, and desired him to
procure one for her ; and also several others had
made the same request.

" Since that date there has been a constant call for
Bibles and Testaments.   Scarcely a day has passed
in which there have not been Mexicans at my door
earnestly soliciting a copy of the Scriptures.   Since
I have been writing this letter, I have put eight
copies into the hands of these benighted people.
May we not hope God's blessing will go along
with them, and that the enlightening influence of
the Divine Spirit will lead their deluded readers to
embrace the salvation they reveal ?   I can but
think that the Spirit of God is moving the hearts of
these people, and inducing them thus eagerly to
seek the truth which is able to save their souls.   It
is a source of unspeakable satisfaction to me to witness this eagerness for the word of God.   No one
can estimate the joyful emotions that it occasions
but those who have felt similar painful solicitude
for immortal souls.   While I hate Popery to detes-

tation, I love the souls it enslaves, and will endure any sacrifice or privation to rescue its wretched subjects from its destructive power. In this work, I believe the Bible to be the most efficient agent. Romanism can not exist in the light of God's word, and where it is disseminated, that terrible form of evil must soon disappear.

"Excuse this digression from the main facts of the object which I designed to present. Do you not think, sir, that the case, as above stated, would justify the sending of a colporteur here? It appears to me that this field presents as urgent motives as any other in the world. I fully believe God will not open the door of Mexico to Protestant laborers until we do what we can for those within our present sphere of influence. Even if no one shall come to my assistance, I shall toil on in faith and hope, believing that though the 'kingdom of God,' in this instance, is but as 'a grain of mustard seed,' yet it may eventually 'grow to be a tree,' whose spreading branches shall prove a blessing to this long-neglected people. And in this belief, I humbly ask the influence and prayers of God's people."

As stated by the Secretary of the American and Foreign Christian Union, an effort was made to procure a suitable man for the field; but after some time of seeking a right kind of a person, I was informed that a *Christian* man, who understood the Spanish, could not be found, and that they were unable to do any thing more. Rather than see such an important work languish for the want of some one to do it, I proposed to the Board of the American and Foreign Christian Union, that if

they would furnish me the means for employing an
assistant teacher in my school, so I could be, in
part, relieved from school duties, I would become
their colporteur and Bible reader. The proposal
was accepted, and January of 1856 I came under
the auspices of that society. Re-enforced by a competent teacher, I was greatly strengthened, and the
school and Bible distribution received a new impulse.
I visited all the houses of the Mexicans in Brownsville and vicinity, and supplied every family of
which any member could read, with a Bible. Only
occasionally would I find one who rejected it. It
was said by my American friends : " The Mexicans
take your Bibles to turn over to the priests to be
burned." I would follow up my investigations
until I was satisfied that such was not true. Indeed,
I never ascertained that a single Bible was destroyed. But *I did* ascertain that the Mexicans concealed them in the most careful manner, taking
them out and reading them by night, as they said,
" when the priests were not about." I went one
day to the house where one of my pupils resided,
to inquire after her absence, and also to make inquiry after a Bible I had furnished her. A report
had crept into school that she had exchanged it with
the nuns for a " saint," and that they (the nuns)
had burned it. The mother of the girl met me at
the door, and with streaming eyes told me that her
daughter had died with yellow fever but a short
time before. I asked her, if she had her Bible ?

She replied, " No, I put her Bible in her coffin, as she loved it so much, and it was buried with her." I found another similar case, where a father had put the Bible by the side of his son in his coffin.   Although I could not fully coincide with this use of God's Word, yet there was something pathetic and suggestive in the act of these bereaved Mexican parents.

Orders would be brought me from Monterey and from places in the interior of Mexico, for dozens of Bibles, with the money to pay for them.   I feared sometimes the priests were behind the scenes, but upon inquiring, Why do you want the Bible? the answer uniformly was, " We have read the Bible, and find it to be a *good* book, and we want to get numbers to distribute among the people gratuitously, to let them see that the priests have deceived them, in telling them that the Bible is not a fit book for them to read."   Through a Protestant German, also, great quantities of evangelical reading were carried far into the interior.   This man was a traveling portrait painter, and the nature of his business gave him access to Mexican families, who gladly received the word of God, and paid him for it.   As this was before the prohibition was removed, he often encountered violent opposition; yet he felt so deeply the spiritual deprivations of Mexico, that he was willing sometimes to run great risks, not only of losing his personal effects, but also his life.   At one time, his hat was taken from

him, and he was obliged to travel some ten miles
or more without any covering for his head; which,
under the scorching rays of a Mexican sun, was no
small deprivation.   He finally lost his life in Mexico; whether he was killed on account of the dis-
semination of the Bible, or for purposes of robbery,
we never ascertained.   It was known that he
stopped for the night at a town named Comer, half
way between Monterey and Matamoras, but nothing
more was ever heard of him by his friends.   He
was eminently a man of God, and, we felt assured,
that like the martyr Stephen, he had " fallen asleep
in Jesus," although a violent death was permitted
to be his.

CHAPTER X.

Troubled waters—A storm of persecution—False impressions
made by enemies—School nearly broken up—Judgments of
God pronounced—Submitting the case to God, and waiting for a manifestation—Sudden removal of the instigator
of the persecution—A great calm ensued—Work resumed
and school full again.

BUT did I sail on smooth waters during these
years of labor among the Romanists of Brownsville? By no means. The spirit of popery was
fully alive, and in violent activity to counteract my
influence. The prosperity of my school was a subject of great annoyance. That Catholics should
choose to send their children to a school which
they, the priests, had denounced from the pulpit as
"the by-way to hell," was not to be tolerated.
The magazine, containing the letter in which I said,
"I hated Romanism," was procured and taken to
the convent to be read and discussed before the
pupils. All the matter contained in it against
popery, and, of course, it was not at all compli-
mentary, was rehearsed as mine; and the impression
was made that I was the author of the book, and
had gone north the year before to write it. The
priests went to the parents of my pupils, and said
to them, " Miss Rankin says she hates Catholics,
why do you permit your children to be taught by
her?" Some of the parents, I knew, replied, " We

can not believe Miss Rankin hates our children; she treats them kindly, giving them clothing and books, and comes to see them when they are sick." Such a combined effort seemed to be made against me, that I greatly feared my seminary building might be destroyed, and several of my friends expressed similar anxiety. In one of my letters to the secretary of the A. & F. C. U., I made allusion to this fear, and he, very injudiciously published it, under the heading, "An attempt made by the Romanists to destroy the Protestant seminary building at Brownsville." With this flaming embellishment the most profound sensation was produced among the priests, who were conversant with the magazine containing the letter, and the statement was heralded through town "that Miss Rankin had been guilty of the grossest falsehoods." The whole place was carried by the impulse. Even the Protestants who had said to me, "we fear for your building," dare not speak in my defense. The Brownsville paper, whose editor, temporarily, was a Roman Catholic, took up the matter, with all its power and influence. The priests went from house to house, among my patrons, and, under the influence of the wild excitement, some of my best Mexican friends took their children from my school. Indeed, I lost more than half my pupils. The very atmosphere seemed filled with curses and imprecations against me, yet I felt shut up in "God's pavilion." It is the "fiery furnace," and the "lion's den," that teach the children of God where their protection and strength lie. Although human nature may shrink from the encounter of the "wrath of man," yet it is declared that the "wrath of man" shall be overruled to the glory of God. I cast myself upon the arm of Omnipotence, and abode in peace under the shadow of the Almighty. I heard, one day, that a Catholic woman, an American, by the way, said with much emphasis, "The judgment of God must come upon Miss Rankin." I immediately replied, "I will also submit the matter to the judgment of God. If I am verily guilty of wrong, as you represent, let divine judgment fall upon my head, but if your party are guilty, let the deserved judgment be passed upon it." I felt assured some manifest token would be given, and waited on God in humble expectation; although the manifestation might be "by terrible things in righteousness." The "Father Superior," who had been the leading spirit in this persecution, was obliged to leave on business connected with a church building they were erecting in Brownsville. After getting every thing arranged against me according to his wishes, he took passage on the steamer Nautilus for New Orleans. The Gulf of Mexico is subject to violent tornadoes at the season of the year in which he took passage, and when the steamer arrived within fifty miles of the South West Pass, a sudden gale struck her, and she went down with all on board, excepting *one* man, who saved himself on a door which floated off

7

with him.   In about ten days news came to Brownsville of the dreadful disaster, and great distress was
felt for the loss of many valuable lives.   Among
the number was the Father Superior, and of course,
his sudden death was a severe blow to his friends.
The lady who had pronounced God's judgment upon
me was the first one, after the arrival of the news,
to catch her prayer book and go to the church to
pray for the father's soul.   All the varieties of
" masses " were brought in requisition for the same
purpose, but whether they obtained peace for the
Father Superior's soul, I have never ascertained.
But peace for my soul was secured, not because a
fellow mortal had been suddenly called from time
into eternity in this fearful manner, but because the
attention of my enemies was diverted from me to
the solemn circumstances of the untimely death of
their adored father.   The waves of persecution were
suddenly checked and a great calm ensued.   I went
around among my Mexican friends, and was warmly
welcomed as their true friend.   In less than two
months my school was full, and I never received
the like persecution again.

CHAPTER XI.

A revolution for religious freedom—The Priest Party and
  Liberal Party—Immense revenues of the church party—
  Juarez, an able leader of the liberal party—The justice of
  the cause gives hope—Letters writted to the A. & F. C. U.
  at that time—The Scriptures going rapidly into Mexico—
  Fifteen hundred copies of the Scriptures, and more than
  two hundred thousand pages of tracts—Great joy in the
  work—Severe affliction and sickness—Touching fidelity
  of a Mexican woman—The bandit Cortinas—Brownsville
  invaded—Four weeks absence in Matamoras—A school
  with New Testaments—Two Mexican women wondering
  why they had ever prayed to saints—Another burning her
  images—They did not keep her son from death—If they
  had known the Bible before they would have believed in
  it—Final triumph of the Liberal party—A great demand
  for Bibles and tracts for Mexico—The American Bible
  and Tract Societies supplying.

IN 1857, a revolution was commenced for religious
freedom in Mexico. The parties engaged were
called "The Church Party" and "The Liberal
Party." The former, wielding the ecclesiastical,
political, civil, military, and monetary powers of
the whole country, possessed advantages which left
to the liberal party but little prospect of ultimate
success. The justice of the cause of the latter
seemed their only hope, and it was a subject of
earnest entreaty to the Author of the human conscience, that divine power would interpose in behalf

of this nation, so long under a government directly opposed to the best interests of the people, either temporal or spiritual. To human view, the hope could scarcely be indulged. With Mirimon, one of the most skillful generals of Mexico, at their head, backed by the clergy, who were rich in resources, the church party was not wanting in worldly power. The priests were said to be the great bankers of Mexico, having entire control of all the church revenues, which were immense. Yet, as "the race is not always to the swift, nor the battle to the strong," we indulged the hope that, ultimately, right would prevail in this eventful struggle. There were men of decided ability in the liberal party. Juarez, with his compatriots, seemed resolute and determined to throw off the ecclesiastical rule, which, like the pall of Egypt, had long overshadowed the land, and establish a government more in harmony with the rights of man and the spirit of modern civilization. Juarez sought the government of the people, by the people and for the people, and endeavored to establish the principle of the direct suffrage of all the citizens in the election of the officers of government. The constitution, embracing the principles of freedom to the Mexican people, was adopted February 8, 1857. Although the clergy were beaten on the field of battle and foiled in congress, they did not despair; but continued their resistance with determined zeal. Juarez, with faith in the people, advanced under all discouragements, for the accomplishment of the object upon which the life of the nation depended. The events transpiring in Mexico greatly encouraged me in the belief that religious freedom would yet prevail in that fair land, and that I could yet plant my foot there with an open Bible in my hand. Can it be possible, I often exclaimed to myself, that I can ever be permitted to follow up those rills of light which have been secretly flowing into that dark land, and personally witness the glorious results? I believed, without a doubt, that there were many hearts which had embraced the blessed truths of the Gospel, as revealed in the Word of God, and were silently praying for additional help from the living teacher. My heart often bounded in joyful anticipation, yet I must yet wait in faith and prayer and work on. An extract of a letter which I wrote to the A. & F. C. U. will give some idea of the progress of the work at this time.

I say, during three months past I have *sold* fifty copies of the Scriptures, several D'Aubigne's History of the Reformation, also six thousand pages of other evangelical reading *in* Mexico. I often feel the truth of these words, " Behold, I have set before you an open door, and no *man* can shut it; for thou hast a little strength, and hast kept my word, and hast not denied my name." We ought to be encouraged while our opportunities of spreading the truth in Mexico is becoming enlarged. So much of the power of the papacy has been compelled to

yield before the light of Divine truth, that we may
well thank God, and take courage.   Every copy of
the Holy Scriptures conveyed into Mexico is pleading for religious liberty.   Where God's Word becomes disseminated, the bolts and bars binding the
human intellect and conscience become dissevered.
In the desperate struggle, now being made in that
land, where popery has so long held the supreme
control, we see the intense desire manifested for the
inalienable rights which God has conferred upon
all his intelligent creatures.   Whether God's time
has fully come for Mexico's redemption is not cer-
tain.   One day we hear of the triumph of the Liberals; the next day, perhaps, the reverse.   Although
victory may be delayed, yet justice and truth will
ultimately triumph in the utter overthrow of error
and priest-craft."

Notwithstanding my brilliant hopes abroad, a
deep shadow was hovering over my happy home
and work.   In September, of 1858, my beloved
sister, who had been my associate teacher for nearly
three years, was suddenly stricken down by yellow
fever.   My grief was most intense, yet not without
abundant hope for her, whose death was most tri-
umphant.   Yet her loss to me, not only for her
companionship, but for the great assistance she rendered me in my work, seemed almost irreparable.
But God's grace proved sufficient in those days of
severe affliction, and I was enabled to go on my

way, under the comforting assurance of my Divine Friend, " Lo, I am with you alway."

The year of 1859 was marked also by some trying experience. In August of that year, I was attacked by yellow fever, and for some time it seemed that I too might have to lay down my armor; and I quietly resigned myself to pass away, if such was the will of my heavenly Father ; but the grief and anxiety manifested by my Mexican friends aroused me to renew my grasp of life, and to ask God to yet spare me for further service in His cause. The kind solicitude of these people made me willing to live longer, if only for their sakes. One incident, I desire to state, showing a phase of character of the Mexican women, which, although not new to me, may serve to illustrate to those less acquainted with them, that " some good may come out of Nazareth." Connected with my school was a family of six children, which I had sought out in my tours around among the Mexican jackals soon after I went to Brownsville ; they were orphans, and were supported by their grandmother and two aunts. Being very poor, and entirely dependent upon their daily labor for the support of these children, I assisted in furnishing them with clothing and books. Their improvement and good conduct amply rewarded me for all I did for them. The morning after my attack of fever, three or four girls came to school, and being informed that I was sick, they asked permission to come to my room.   It was granted, and they came and stood beside my bed, and seemed much distressed.   They then went home, crying aloud, and besought their grandmother (who was an experienced nurse) "to go and take care of Miss Rankin, and not let her die."   The grandmother came immediately to my house, related what the children had said, and offered to stay and take care of me. I very readily accepted her offer, as I had only two young girls in my house, and sickness, at that time, was prevailing so extensively in town, that no dependence could be placed upon friends and neighbors.   This Mexican woman remained, and nursed me as kindly as a mother could have done, following with the utmost precision all the orders of my physician, putting aside her roots and herbs, remedies used by the Mexicans for similar cases.   After some days of unremitting care, she came to me one morning, saying she had received a call to go and nurse three strangers who had been stricken with the prevailing fever, with the offer of fifteen dollars a day, as the case was a most urgent one. I said, you will go, will you not? and urged her to do so, as I knew their need of money.   She replied, most emphatically, "I shall not leave you until I know you are past all danger, to go and take care of others, although they will pay me so much.   But," added she, "I have too much gratitude in my heart for what you have done for me and mine, to take any pay for what I have done for you; I shall not leave you;" nor did she, until she was perfectly satisfied that I needed her services no longer.

My experience with the Mexicans has proved that they are a kind **people**, if treated with kindness. I can truly say I have never found firmer and better friends among any nation of people than I have among some of the Mexicans. Many, very many, I shall never cease to love and respect while life remains.

Scarcely had the pestilence ceased its work of devastation when new dangers threatened Brownsville. The notorious Cortinas commenced **his** career of lawlessness in September of **that** year, which he has continued upon that frontier, by deeds of murder and robbery, with unremitting energy, until the present time. Cortinas was American born, and had been somewhat of an extensive land owner on the Texan side of the Rio Grande. It has been said that he was a quiet and inoffensive citizen, until he conceived the **idea**, whether justly or not, that he had been wronged by some of the Americans of Brownsville in regard to his property. He resolved, it seems, to take their lives, as he said "he could get redress in **no other** way." The United States troops, by order of General Twiggs, being withdrawn from the frontier, the way was prepared for Cortinas to carry into execution his murderous design. **He** collected some sixty Mexicans, of like character with himself, and he with them, on the morning of the 28th September, entered the town, and announced their arrival by the discharge of muskets, and taking their position in the center of the town, proclaimed "Death to the Americans." They then proceeded to the work they had announced by murdering several prominent citizens. Their victims were already selected, and they went to their houses and called them out, and when they came, which they would do, unsuspectingly, they were killed in the presence of their families.

As soon as possible the citizens organized themselves into a body for defense; but only about one hundred and fifty men could be found who were regarded as trustworthy. One of the merchants happened to have a quantity of arms on hand, so they were tolerably well equipped for defense. Cortinas intrenched himself a short distance from town, awaiting his opportunity of coming in and completing his work of death. He was re-enforced in a short time with additional recruits, so that his numbers exceeded ours. It was only by the utmost vigilance and intrepidity of the citizens that this murderous band was repelled. By day and by night our men were compelled to stand on constant guard, until they became almost worn out. Cortinas endeavored to cut off all communication, yet with much difficulty a courier eluded his ambush, and succeeded in getting to the capitol and informing the Governor of the State of our perilous con-

dition. Troops were immediately sent to our relief, and Cortinas was compelled to withdraw his
band of desperadoes.

For two weeks after the assault of Cortinas I remained in my house and continued my school, as
I knew his murderous designs were only against
his enemies. As long as he had his own band of
men, who were fully instructed upon whom to
commit violence, I felt no apprehensions that any
harm would befall me. But when he was re-enforced by desperadoes from all parts, I became convinced that I should be in danger in case they succeeded in getting into the town. I went to Matamoras, and remained three or four weeks. Although invited to stay with an American family, I
preferred taking up my abode with a Mexican
woman, whom I had known considerably by having supplied her with Bibles, from time to time,
for distribution in Matamoras. This woman had
come to me upon the first attack of Cortinas, and
invited me to come to her house, so when I felt
there was real danger, I gladly accepted her
proffered hospitality. She had supplied many of
her friends with books, and my stay with her gave
me an opportunity of ascertaining their influence.
I was much gratified by finding among them an
evident appreciation of the word of God. Many
said, "If we had known the Bible before, we
would have believed it."

I found also a whole school, of some thirty boys,

supplied with the New Testament, which they daily read. The teacher, who was an elderly Mexican man, had a Bible, which he had procured many years before from a British vessel lying in a Mexican port. I visited his school, and he expressed great gratitude to me for furnishing him, so as to enable him to put a copy of the blessed book into the hands of all his pupils. He told me he had learned from the Bible to cast away his idols and to trust in Christ for salvation. The Mexican woman told me that this man, in speaking of me, was accustomed to call me "sister," and I was pleased to reciprocate the appellation by recognizing in him a brother in Christ.

Image worship, I found, was decreasing under the light of Divine Truth. I heard two Mexican women conversing one day in a manner which indicated that their faith was somewhat shaken in the "saints," whose pictures hung upon the walls of the room. One of the women said to the other, "How foolish it is for us to pray to such things," pointing to the images, and added, in the most emphatic manner, "Why do we do so?" The other woman replied in the same manner, "Why do we?" One woman, with whom I became acquainted, told me she had burned all her images, as they failed to render her any help in times of trouble. She had lost her husband by death, and soon after her only son, a man grown, lay at the point of death with the fever. She said she had several important saints to which she had been accustomed to pay her daily devotions, and of course she appealed to them for help in this hour of anguish. She offered them all her property, which was considerable, for the Church, if they would interpose and save her beloved son from death. But, as she said, "They paid no heed to my distresses, and let my son die." In perfect contempt and indignation she broke them to pieces and threw them into the fire, except *one*, which she kept as a memorial, being a bridal gift of her late husband.

Many hearts in Mexico, I felt assured, yearned for a religion which should meet the wants of their souls. How often, during those years in which I witnessed those aspirations for a more exalted source of consolation, did I cry out in agony of soul, "How long, O Lord, how long ere thou wilt arise and avenge the blood of thy servants which is shed?" How long shall human laws shut out the true light, which is intended to enlighten every soul of our fallen race, even that of the poor despised Mexican! "Shall not the prey be taken from the mighty, and the suffering captive be delivered?"

Thus saith the Lord, "Even the captives of the mighty *shall* be taken away, and the prey of the terrible *shall* be delivered; for I will contend with him that contendeth with thee, and I will save thy children."

Near the close of 1859, a light finally dawned

upon the long night of darkness in Mexico. On the 25th December, Juarez and the Liberal Party entered the Capital. The night before it had been abandoned by Mirimon and the remnant of his completely demoralized and conquered army.

Was not this a bright era in Mexican history? "The gates of brass" were broken in pieces, "the bars of iron were cut in sunder," and eight millions of souls threw off the shackels of popery and emerged into the liberty wherewith God makes his people free. The popular demonstrations—the ringing of bells and firing of cannon by the people generally evinced their great joy for the precious boon of religious liberty. As the noise from Matamoras broke upon my ear, I thought I never heard more delightful sounds, and my heart bounded in joyful anticipation that God's Word could now have free course, run, and be glorified.

Men came over immediately from Matamoras for Bibles and Tracts, saying, "We can now distribute Protestant books without any hinderance, and we will pay you for all you can let us have." I supplied them to the extent of my ability, and wrote on to the Bible and Tract Societies for a greater supply.

CHAPTER XII.

Wrote to the Bible Society for an Agent—Rev. Mr Thompson
receives an appointment—Goes into Mexico—Brings two
Mexicans to Brownsville, who unite with the Protestant
Church—First fruits—Work interrupted by civil war in
the United States—Desirous of going to Monterey—French
intervention and civil war prevented—Rev. Mr. Hickey
appointed agent for the Bible Society—Scatters Bibles over
the country—The French intervention threatens Protestantism—Maximilian and Carlotta—Maximilian's fluctua-
tions—Carlotta's insanity—The Pope refuses assistance to
Maximilian — French troops withdrawn — Maximilian
finally executed—Religious freedom nobly outrides the
storm.

AFTER a few months of constant demands for
Bibles and other evangelical books, I came to
the conclusion that a special agent was required,
and that the American Bible Society would be
justified in putting one into this waiting and needy
field. Although I felt it to be almost a personal
favor, I resolved to make the request; and to make
it sure as possible I secured the man, whom I
thought would serve acceptably, as already possessing some acquaintance with the Mexicans and their
language. Rev. Mr. Thompson, who had been sent
by the Methodist Episcopal Church South, to labor
on the Rio Grande, assented to my proposition, and
I wrote to the secretary for an appointment for him

to labor in Mexico.   After some little delay to make the necessary inquiries of the conference which sent Mr. T. of his character and fitness, he received an appointment and commenced his duties in October, 1860.   He went into Mexico, and, as I expected, was received with favor.   He was told by the authorities that he might preach, plant schools, build churches, disseminate the Bible, and do any thing that would benefit the people.

He went as far as Monterey, and found the Bible had preceded him, and had been read by many to advantage.   At Cadereyta, a place thirty miles from Monterey, he met a man, who, as soon as he saw him, inquired, "Are you not a teacher of the Bible." "I have dreamed of just such a looking man as you; I knew there must be somewhere the living teacher of that book."   Mr. Thompson found this man well acquainted with the Scriptures.   He wrote me, he rarely found a man in a Protestant community who was more familiar with the Word of God than this Mexican.   He comprehended those passages which we believe to apply to the Church of Rome; had discarded the whole system of popery; and embraced the religion of the Bible, and gave evidence of being truly " born again." When Mr. Thompson returned to Brownsville in March, 1861, this man and his eldest son came with him, and, after due examination, were received into a Protestant Church.   These were the *first* Mexicans who durst come out and publicly profess the Protestant faith. The fact being proven that a Mexican *could* be otherwise than a Catholic; others followed; and it was an unspeakable satisfaction to give the right hand of Christian fellowship to people from a nation which had been regarded as beyond the reach of a pure Christianity. Indeed, I rejoiced, believing these first fruits were an earnest of the harvest which faith had bid me expect, and I doubted not that many more precious souls would be gathered from those dark dominions of error and superstition into the true fold of Christ.

Mr. Thompson continued his labors with hopeful success until the civil war in the United States prevented our having communication with the North. The Southern ports were all blockaded, and among them the port of Brazos, and we could obtain no more Bibles from New York. Mr. Thompson came to Brownsville, and after waiting some time for a change of affairs, finally concluded to leave the work and return to Texas.

It seemed Bible work in Mexico had received a sudden check; yet I still trusted in the same Right Arm, which had hitherto often interposed in behalf of the perishing millions of that unfortunate country. I did not trust in vain, for a few months later a port was opened on the Mexican side of the Rio Grande, and we were again in communication with the Bible Society of New York. About the same time, Rev. James Hickey, colporteur of the American Tract Society for Texas, on account of being a

"Union man," was obliged to flee to Mexico to
preserve his life, as all persons in the South had to
do at that time, who were loyal to the Government
of the United States. Mr. Hickey came to Matamoras, and seeing the good work already in progress
there, entered into it most heartily. He came over
to Brownsville and I supplied him with Bibles, and
he not only circulated the Word, but preached it,
in all its saving power. Having acquired some
knowledge of the Spanish language in Western
Texas, he was able to preach to the people under-
standingly. Seeing his zeal and adaptation to the
work, with his consent I wrote on to the Bible
Society for his appointment as Agent for Mexico.
In consequence of the irregularity of the mails, Mr.
H. did not receive an appointment until the summer of 1863. He had, however, gone to Monterey
in anticipation of his acceptance by the Bible
Society, and found a promising field of labor. He
collected a congregation of Mexicans, and soon
baptized several, who gave evidence of conversion.
At Cadareyta also he found some who had evidently
embraced the truth in the love of it, by reading the
Bible alone. A Mexican woman said, she had been
seeking, by the strictest observance of all the require-
ments of the Catholic Church, comfort to her soul;
but never found it, until she read, in the New
Testament, of Christ and his salvation; and this
was previous to any Protestant teacher going
there.

As Mr. Hickey's legitimate duties were, according to the rules of the Bible Society, the distribution and sale of the scriptures, he did not remain long in Monterey, but put the work there into the hands of one of the converts,* and went out scattering the Word of Life broadcast over the surrounding country. The eagerness with which many received the Bible from him was truly encouraging.

I should have gone to Monterey immediately after religious liberty was proclaimed, but various things hindered me. I could procure no suitable person to whom I could commit the seminary at Brownsville, and I hesitated to leave until I could. The difficulties arising from the French intervention in Mexico, also rendered it quite impracticable for me to go; as at one time Protestantism seemed to be dangerously threatened. After the occupation of Mexico by the Liberals, Mirimon and the other leaders of the church party, went to France and represented the country as having thrown off all restraint, and being in a state of absolute anarchy, and that, unless some power intervened, it would go to utter ruin. Napoleon III. conceived that this representation might serve as a pretext for getting possession of Mexico; and, as a civil war was prevailing in the United States, he very reasonably supposed he should receive no hinderance from the American government.

---

* Thomas Westrup, a young Englishman, who had been converted through Mr. H.'s instrumentality.

He decided to improve the opportunity presented by establishing an empire in Mexico, and proposed to Maximilian to go and take the imperial throne. At first Maximilian objected, his refusal being founded upon reasons very satisfactory to himself. But Carlotta, being a staunch Catholic, conceived that the proposal for her husband to go to Mexico " was a call from heaven to go and restore the fallen church." Maximilian was finally prevailed upon to come to Mexico, and, it is fully believed, with the purpose and hope of benefiting the country and people. He was, evidently, greatly deceived, both by Napoleon and the Mexican representatives. The true facts of the case can not better be presented than by using the precise words of the Abbe Domenech, French chaplain, who came to Mexico with Maximilian. He says:

" Every thing was a delusion. Unhappily, there were a great many interested parties. However, be that as it may, we were deceived on every side, and urged on, if not by a chivalric sentiment like that which led us to take up arms for the Christians in Syria and for the independence of the Italians, at least by a sentiment of high policy France entered upon Mexico, and substituted in favor of the Archduke Maximilian, a monarchy for a republican regime." But it proved a failure.

The falsity of Miramon's representations and the absurdity of Carlotta's conceptions were fully proved when Maximilian, upon his arrival, found the great

majority of the Mexican people opposed to a foreign
intervention, and also to the re-establishment of the
church party. Although there still existed remnants
of such a party in Mexico, yet it was much in the
minority. And when Maximilian, instigated by
the pope, demanded that the immense revenues
which formerly belonged to the church should be
restored, it was found that the Liberals had such
absolute possession as precluded all hope of ever
obtaining them. A complication of difficulties beset Maximilian, yet he persevered under them all.
He prohibited the Protestant religion, and for a
time Mr. Hickey durst not go out upon his work.
But the people were determined to resist the reign-
ing power, and the emperor, finding that the great
majority of the people were in favor of a religious
freedom, decided to turn over to that side, hoping
probably, by so doing, to win them into favor with
the empire which he vainly was trying to establish.
But he found they were no more willing to become
subjects of his imperial reign than they were to
submit to religious despotism. Mirimon, and
others who had been his friends, deserted him and
left the country.

The pope issued all the denunciations against him
of which his infallible personage was capable, but
Maximilian stood firm, daring to reply to him that
he "believed toleration to all religions, which were
not against morality and civilization, were essential
to the prosperity of any country." This was a

bright spot in Maximilian's career in Mexico, and I shall always remember him with grateful appreciation for the firm defense of those principles upon which the welfare of Mexico depended.

But the situation of the Emperor Maximilian was far from being pleasant. With enemies within and foes without, he sailed on a sea of troubles. Napoleon, who had been the instrumentality of placing him in this situation, suddenly announced his intention of withdrawing the French troops from Mexico, alleging that the empire was so well established that foreign assistance was no longer necessary. Whether he really indulged this absurd belief is extremely doubtful, as the real facts entirely disproved the supposition. It is more probable that the fear of the United States moved him to recall his troops, as our government had so far overcome its own difficulties as to be able to look after those of its neighbors. Demonstrations were clearly manifested that the United States would not permit the permanent lodgment of a monarchial government upon this continent, and Napoleon did not feel quite willing to fall into its power, already distinguished for victorious combat with powerful enemies.

Carlotta, with woman's instinct, seeing the fatal sonsequences to the interests of the empire, should it cease to be sustained by foreign bayonets, flew to France, and entreated Napoleon to forbear his threatened purpose. Not prevailing with him, she went to the Vatican, and besought the holy father to exercise his power in behalf of the falling empire. The pope, still sore, no doubt, from Maximilian's arrogance in opposing his pontifical orders in relation to matters with regard to which Mexico was of importance to him, turned a deaf ear to her appeals.

This denial actually wrought the destruction of the lovely Carlotta's reason. Her brain received a fatal shock, and she was carried from the Vatican a hopeless maniac. As might be expected, when the French troops left Mexico, Maximilian was entirely without support. And why did he not leave with the retiring army? It will always be a matter of deep regret that he did not leave Mexico at that time; for although his fair fame might have been somewhat tarnished by his unsuccessful attempt to establish an imperial throne, yet, by so doing, he would have been spared to his friends and to his country yet longer.

He remained, however, and suffered himself to become again the dupe of Mirimon and others, who, at this juncture, turned up again in Mexico. They represented that immense wealth was yet in possession of the church party, and Maximilian was led to believe that there was sufficient power for sustaining him at the head of the Empire. In accepting the support of the church party, he abjured the principles which he had so boldly declared in favor of religious freedom. This was a dark blot upon his integrity and honor. Probably his extremity forced him to fall into the plan. In his first attempt for carrying it into execution, he fell into a fatal trap, and, with Mirimon and Mejia, expiated, by an ignominious death, the wicked design of again enslaving the millions of Mexico under papal dominion.

No one can fail to lament the sacrifice of the life of this good-hearted, yet evidently weak-headed, man, nor deplore the mental ruin of " poor Carlotta," who still lives—a monument of disappointed ambition.

This great sacrifice can be clearly traced to the unwise design of Napoleon, who laid the treacherous snare which lured two innocent victims on to ruin. But as he has passed to a higher tribunal, human judgment should leave him there. Religious freedom, however, nobly outrode the storm, overcoming the plots and counterplots of the most potent enemies, and Mexico presented the same hopeful aspect for missionary work as before.

CHAPTER XIII.

WHILE these events were taking place in Mexico I was having some varied, yet rich experience on the frontier. In September of 1862 I was obliged to leave my seminary and work in Brownsville, by the most peremptory orders. The orders were sent me in writing by a Presbyterian minister, who stated that he was authorized to command me to vacate the building, and deliver up the keys of the same to him.

I replied that I wished to retain the seminary for the purposes for which I founded it—namely, the education of Mexican children—and put the question, "Why do you require me to give it up?" He replied, in a written statement, "You are not in sympathy with the Southern Confederacy, and no teachers but such as are can be permitted to occupy that institution;" also, "You are in commu-

9 .

nication with a country called the United States."
I again remonstrated, and continued to occupy the
building which I had procured at such an immense
amount of labor and sacrifice until another written
order* came, announcing it to be the "third and
last"—evidently meaning that violence would have
to be used if I did not voluntarily vacate the premises.

Rather than be put out by military force, which
I fully believed this man would call into requisition, I wrote a reply that, in obedience to his command, I would commit the building and all its responsibilities into his hands, and that I would leave
him in the hands of Him who has said, "Judgment
and justice are the habitation of my throne."

Through the aid of friends I succeeded in getting
over to Matamoras, with my books, furniture, etc.,
although the rebel minister went to the Confederate
receiver and urged him to confiscate all my mova-
ble possessions. The receiver reported this fact to
me himself; and although a Roman Catholic, he
said he told my Protestant friend it was bad enough
for *man* to be afflicted with the horrors of war, and
that he could not have the heart to extort from a
woman her necessary articles of furniture.

I succeeded in procuring a house, and opened a
school in Matamoras, and was supremely happy in
engaging in actual labor for Mexicans upon Mexi-

---

* The documents are still preserved.

can soil. This was the time of the difficulties prevailing in Mexico, and I could not feel it prudent
to go farther into the country. I remained in Matamoras until March of 1863, when I could not procure a house on any terms. The great quantities
of goods which passed through Bagdad, the new
port that was opened for the benefit of the Southern
Confederacy, were stored in Matamoras, and every
available building was required for that purpose.
It was not unfrequently the case that a hundred
vessels were lying off the bar; not only were they
discharging goods, but were receiving large quantities of cotton for foreign ports. On account of
the prevailing troubles of both countries, I felt it
best to discontinue any further work for Mexico
until matters became more settled. I concluded to
go to New Orleans, which was then occupied by
the Federals, and proceed to the North. A United
States transport was sent from New Orleans to convey refugees, who had fled from the South at the
peril of their lives, and were waiting in Matamoras
for an opportunity to get to the United States. I
took passage, and, with my two nieces, and two
other families in company, went to Bagdad, where
the vessel was lying. A very difficult bar obstructed the entrance; and just before we arrived
a "norther" sprang up, which rendered the bar so
rough that it was utterly impossible for us to cross;
consequently we were compelled to seek for quarters in Bagdad until the gale ceased.

It was night when we arrived, and we went immediately to the place called a hotel. We were informed by the proprietors that no accommodations could be afforded us, and we walked out and stood outside, utterly at a loss what to do. We understood the reason why we were not permitted to remain in the hotel, as it was well known that Bagdad had been reared especially for the rebels, and was noted for its deep-seated hatred of "Yankees," as all Union people were called in those days.

While we were standing outside, exposed to the bleak winds of a Mexican "norther," a young man came along, and kindly invited us to go on board a small schooner which was lying inside of the bar. The young man, who was a Nova Scotian, said he heard the refusal of the hotel-keepers, and he thought, "What if my mother and sisters were in the like situation!" and the thought impelled him to offer us such accommodations as he was able.

We very thankfully accepted his invitation, and accompanied him to the schooner; yet we found very limited accommodations for our party, which consisted of eight persons. We could scarcely stand upright, and as for our lodgings, barrels, boxes, and the like, constituted our beds. We passed the night with considerable amusement, in our crude attempts to obtain rest. The morning came, and in our attempts to obtain breakfast we found the rebels determined not to let the "Yankees" have any thing to eat. By strategy, however, our kind friends of the schooner succeeded in obtaining something which answered for a breakfast.

The bar continued rough, and we were compelled to remain, and we made several futile attempts during the day to secure more commodious quarters; but were finally compelled to remain on the little schooner another night. The day following, the owner of a larger schooner hearing of our situation, offered to let us come on board his vessel provided we would occupy the hold. He was a Northern man, but was making money off the Confederates, and he did not like to jeopardize his lucrative business by having it known that he was manifesting any favor to Union people. We accepted his invitation, and took up our quarters in our novel apartment, which the owner had somewhat prepared, by having it swept but not "garnished."

Our furniture consisted of a small wood-pile, a bale of cotton, and some ropes and sails. The latter served for our lodgings, which proved to be not the most downy beds that ever were; yet we felt thankful for even these accommodations. We remained nine days in this condition; the owner of the vessel furnishing us with food, and treating us as well as circumstances would permit. Indeed, I shall always retain a grateful remembrance of this man's kindness and hospitality to us.

Our stay was prolonged by a highly outrageous

act of the rebels upon some of our party who were waiting to cross over to the transport. A band of rebels, led by a prominent confederate officer, came over upon the Mexican side of Rio Grande during the night, and took two prominent Union men, bound them, and carried them across the river into the camp of the rebels. These two men were refugees from Texas—one was Judge Davis, late Governor of Texas, and the other, Captain Montgomery, who had been obliged to flee, leaving a wife and several children behind in Texas. These men were immediately started for Brownsville, and when about half way Captain Montgomery was hung, and his head cut off and carried to Brownsville as a trophy. Judge Davis was left at a camp, near town, probably for further sacrifice. In the meantime, intelligence was conveyed to Matamoras of the outrage committed upon Mexican soil, and the outrage was of a more aggravating character from the fact that Judge Davis had been taken from the house of the chief officer of the Mexican government where he had put himself for protection. The Governor, exceedingly incensed, demanded the restoration of the men, or he would immediately stop all transportation of goods across the Rio Grande. This threat was heeded, and Judge Davis was restored, but Captain Montgomery had already fallen a victim to Confederate cruelty, and his family was left in desolation and sorrow. Oh! those were bloody times in

Texas, and can the stains of those tragic scenes ever be effaced? Even though the lapse of years may throw them far in the distance, yet the deeds which were committed during that awful reign of terror, memory can never cease to recall, however painful it may be.

But, I will return to our transport waiting outside the bar. When this daring outrage was committed, an officer who was at Bagdad, ventured, at the risk of his life, to cross over to the vessel, and give information to the captain, who put out immediately for Galveston to procure a gunboat, for resisting any further assault which might be made by the rebels.

In four days after, the vessel returned, and the bar became sufficiently smooth for crossing, so we passed out of our dismal quarters, and went on to the Transport, truly happy to find ourselves again under the dear old " Stars and Stripes " of our own beloved country. Our vessel, originally used for the transportation of cattle, did not prove to be very comfortable. Our party, consisting of about one hundred refugees, found accommodations to be somewhat limited. But, during those days of national peril, all who truly loved our country, and sympathized in its dangers, were as one family— our interests so blending that each one felt like helping and comforting the other.

We arrived at the mouth of the Mississippi the evening of the fifth day, and from one of the gun-

boats lying there came a gentleman on to our vessel, who occupied an important position in the
army, and who urged me to stop in New Orleans,
saying that Union ladies were greatly needed there
at that time.

CHAPTER XIV.

New work presented—Visiting the hospitals—Delicacies solic-
ited in New Orleans—Personal distribution of them—
Scenes of suffering—Principal of school for Freedmen—
An old preacher learning the alphabet—Manifestations of
Divine grace—Desirous of returning to my Mexican work.

I HAD fully intended going to the North, and
getting away from anxious care for a season,
but upon further consideration I decided to remain
in New Orleans. A residence was immediately
furnished me, and I soon became very comfortably
domiciled in the Crescent City. Various ways of
usefulness opened before me, but I felt the most
important work to be, if possible, to aid our country's cause. Indeed, it seemed to be *the* work at
that time, and I felt that every other consideration
should be subordinate.

The siege of Port Hudson was soon in progress,
and hundreds of our brave men were brought to
New Orleans wounded in the most shocking manner. The 27th May, 1863, was marked by one of
those futile attempts to take the fort—the only result of which was the massacre of great numbers
of soldiers. Some three hundred of those who
could be moved were brought down on a steamer
the day after the battle. The scene of their removal from the boat to the St. James Hospital was

related to me by an eye-witness. I was moved at
the recital, and immediately resolved that I would
do something for the comfort of these mutilated
men. I did not know as I should be permitted to
visit the hospital, as no ladies could obtain passes
on account of the insolence of rebel ladies, who
had, some time previous, been visitors of the Confederate sick who were prisoners in the hospital. I
was aware of this fact, yet I thought I would
make the effort, for the sake of those suffering soldiers. As belonging to "Banks' Expedition" I
knew they had left their New England homes only
the autumn before, and I thought of those left behind—wives, mothers, and sisters—of the intense
suffering and anxiety which would be theirs did
they but know of the dreadful condition of their
loved ones. I resolved to try and get access, and
as soon as the proper time arrived, I hastened to
the hospital and inquired of the sentinel at the
door if I could see the surgeon in charge. He replied he had been very busy, all the afternoon,
dressing wounds, but he would send and ascertain.
A messenger was dispatched, and very soon the
surgeon made his appearance.

I very promptly explained the object of my visit,
and, looking at me very sharply, he asked me, "Are
you not a northern lady." I replied, "I am."
Then he put the question, very emphatically, "Are
you for the Union?" I told him, I believed I
was, and that the rebels thought so too, as I had

but recently been expelled from their dominions.
After my nationality and politics were settled, which,
at that time, were of the utmost importance, the
surgeon asked me, "In what *way* would you pro-
pose relief for our wounded and sick soldiers?" I
gave him one evidence of my "Yankee" character
in answering his question by asking another. I
inquired, "Are the delicacies provided necessary for
the comfort of the men?" (This was before the
ample provision was made by the Christian Commission.) He replied, "No, but what can you do
in this way?" I said, "I will go out and solicit
donations for that purpose from the citizens of New
Orleans." The surgeon said, "It might be a good
way of testing the loyalty of the present residents,
as, but a short time previous, all who would not
take the oath of allegiance to the United States
government had been requested to leave the city—
those remaining were professedly Union people."

The plan was decided upon, and the surgeon requested me to come to the hospital the next morning, and we would devise the proper method of carrying it into execution. Accordingly, at 10 o'clock
next day, I and my two nieces were at the hospital
to receive instructions and proper authority for
making our Union friends of New Orleans a call.
All necessary arrangements being made, we started
out upon our work of mercy, and found many who
very readily contributed money, or other things
equally valuable. As I expected, some would have

gladly been excused from giving any thing to "Yankee soldiers," but as their refusal might testify that their professed allegiance to the Union government was not so much for the love they had for it, as for the preservation of their own private interests, they gave something from policy, probably.

At 4 o'clock in the afternoon we returned to the hospital with our supplies. The steward very kindly proposed to relieve us from the labor of their distribution, as he and the nurses could administer them. This offer did not strike me favorably. As several persons had suggested that possibly the needy men might not receive the gifts, I had pledged my word that I would see that every thing given should find its desired end. I remonstrated against the proposal of the steward; but he seemed to think he had some authority in the matter, and to test it, I sent for the surgeon in charge. He came and said, "By all means, ladies, go through the wards and distribute the things yourselves. Those suffering men will be cheered by *seeing* ladies who feel so much interest in their welfare—your *personal* visit will be as welcome as your gifts."

With the surgeon in company we started upon our rounds; but oh! how shall I describe the painful scenes, which, after the lapse of years, are still vivid! Some we found beyond the hope of recovery—one poor fellow, whose lungs had been penetrated by a ball, was just gasping for breath, but was able to say, "How much comfort it is to see kind ladies who feel for us in our suffering!" Another, whose throat was pierced by a bullet, could not utter a word, but a look of thankful recognition was even more expressive. It seemed to me that every form of suffering humanity was presented, and once my feelings gave way, and I exclaimed, in agony of spirit, "I can not longer endure the sight of so much suffering!" One of my nieces exclaimed, "Do, aunt, go forward for the sake of the relief you may be able to afford." I rallied, and continued to endure the painful ordeal until every ward was visited. We administered restoratives to those who could receive them. Indeed, there was not one who could not receive a small quantity of the choice cordials which we happily possessed. When I told these men, who had but recently left their New England homes, that I too was a New Englander, their joy was unbounded; and one young soldier, who was from my native town, nearly bounded from his pillow, when informed of the fact.

For three hours we wended our way through these scenes of sorrow and of joy—for there was some pleasure mingled with the pain—and at sunset we returned to our home. Did I sleep that night? No, for my mind was too much occupied with the scenes I had witnessed; yet the sorrowful retrospect was mitigated by the pleasure of believing that some comfort had been imparted to those suffering soldiers. From day to day we continued; alternating, obtaining supplies one day and administering them the next, which plan lessened the oppressiveness of the labor.

Previous to the surrender of Vicksburg, which opened Port Hudson, the vain attempts to take the latter filled every hospital in New Orleans to the utmost extent, and every hotel, excepting the St. Charles, was used for hospital purposes. At one time, sufficient material for bandages was not possessed, and the ladies were appealed to for aid. During the hot sun of June days, I traversed the streets of New Orleans, calling at the houses of ladies of wealth, asking them for material to dress the wounds of our soldiers. I was often repulsed by ladies who would say, "The Yankees have no business to come here and get wounded, and I shall give nothing for them." But I would say, "They are here among you and are suffering, and will not mercy prompt you to give a piece of old linen, or even cotton, which I know you can easily spare?" By continued importunity I generally succeeded in obtaining something, although reluctantly given.

I continued visiting the hospitals until there was no longer any absolute necessity; and in the autumn of 1863, I gave my assistance to the establishment of the first schools for the freedmen. I accepted the appointment as principal of a school in a Presbyterian church of the Third District. In this work I had some new experience. Although I had taught among a people quite as ignorant as the negro race, yet I had never found among any people such an ardent desire for instruction as among this race, who had been born and raised in a civilized and Christian land, yet had no knowledge of the first rudiments of education. Some highly interesting cases came under my observation.

One man who presented himself as a pupil, said, " I am sixty years old and have been a preacher of the Gospel forty years," and yet did not know one letter of the alphabet. He related to me his religious experience, which had constituted the subject of his preaching. He says, " When I thought myself sinking down into eternal woe, due my sins, there appeared One before my eyes who showed me his pierced hands and side, and said, 'All this I suffered that you might be saved from the punishment of your sins.' Oh, I fell down at the feet of this loving Savior, and he raised me up, saying, ' Thy sins are forgiven thee.' I went to others and told them of this loving Jesus, and I can not tell you of the great numbers who have been brought to feel themselves sinners, and made to rejoice in the same forgiving love. I still tell the wonderful story, and though it was forty years ago I first learned the Savior's love, it is still new."

Even so, my sable brother, this story of the " Savior's love" will continue to be *new* when " forty " millions of years have rolled their rounds, and this story of the Gospel of the Son of God is destined to bring in all God's chosen ones, and will never lose its power on earth, " till all the ransomed church of

God be saved to sin no more." How was I struck with the measure of this poor ignorant colored man's labors for Christ and for souls! I doubt not but in the great day he will be able to present more jewels for his master's crown than thousands of others of Christ's people, endowed with all the advantages of human learning.

I found among many of those people some wonderful manifestations of divine grace in their behalf, and I felt convinced that their deprivations had been compensated by a greater measure of the Holy Spirit's power and influence. I should have liked to continue in this work, but I was already committed to one of equal importance, and waited for the way to open for my return to my divinely appointed field of labor.

CHAPTER XV.

Brownsville taken **by the** United States troops—The garrison burned—Attempt to burn the town—Return to Brownsville—Find **the** Seminary building greatly injured—Repaired it, and opened my school—Religious influence of the army—Troops recalled—Obliged to leave—Return to New Orleans—Maximilian decides to sustain religious liberty in Mexico—Start for Monterey—Another visit **to** Bagdad—Close of the war—What the people of Bagdad thought—Assassination of President Lincoln—Disrespectful demonstrations forbidden by **the Confederate General** of Brownsville—Arrived **safely in Monterey.**

IN November of '63, General Banks took Brownsville, and my seminary building was restored to me again.   Early in '64 I crossed the Gulf and took possession, but found it considerably damaged **by** the explosion of gun-powder.   The Confederates were taken by surprise, having no suspicion that the Federals were approaching, until they landed at Brazos.   Of course but a short time was given them for evacuation, in the accustomed way.   Every thing must be destroyed, and the commanding general immediately ordered the garrison to be set on fire, and to facilitate the destruction of the town, gun-powder was placed in such a manner as to make quick work of **it.**   By a **sudden** change of wind **only a** few buildings of the town were burned, but those which remained were more or less damaged by the explosion of the powder. The walls of the seminary, being of brick, were cracked in several places, and all the windows were broken.

I expended two hundred dollars of my own private means for repairs, and opened my school, and soon had sixty pupils. The occupation of Brownsville by the Federal army greatly improved the character of the town. That the presence of an army should cause an increase of moral and religious influences is quite an uncommon circumstance. Several of the officers were Christian men, and, with the chaplains and agents of the Christian Commission, quite a religious community was constituted. During the spring of '64, a hopeful revival of religion prevailed, and many conversions took place among the soldiers. The churches were made vocal every night of the week with songs of praise, and Brownsville, for that time at least, bore the impress of a God-worshiping people. Is it not true, that there was a very decided religious aspect throughout the whole army? Many of our soldiers went into the army thoughtless and unconcerned about their souls, but came out decided Christians.

I was much interested in the conversion of a young Irishman at Brownsville, who was a Roman Catholic before joining the army. He thanked his God that he enlisted as a soldier, as through the Bible and other means of grace he had learned about a religion which did " his soul good." It was pleasant living in Brownsville in those days, and it was with the most painful emotions that we were apprized of the necessity of evacuating and leaving the town again in the hands of the Confederates. The defeat of General Banks up the Red River, made it necessary that the troops occupying Brownsville should be withdrawn for service in the locality of the disaster. This order to us in Brownsville was a sad and most unexpected event, and I am fully aware no event of the war occasioned more pain to me personally than to be obliged again to surrender my work and turn over my repaired house into the hands of those whom I know would treat it with sacrilegious abuse. I even appealed to some of the Confederates to know if I could not be permitted to remain and continue my school. I was told, I should probably receive abuse and insult, so I submitted to the imperative necessity of again breaking up my establishment.*

General Herron, who was in command, rendered me all necessary assistance, and furnished me, with

---

* After the war closed the seminary in Brownsville was occupied by Mrs. Jeremiah Porter, whose husband was agent of the Christian Commission. Mrs. Porter carried on the school very successfully for several years. When Rev. Mr. Porter was sent to Fort Sill, as Chaplain of the United States Army, the seminary was committed to the care of the Presbytery of Western Texas, and it is hoped that the building will still continue to subserve the object for which it was founded.

other ladies, means of transportation to New Orleans. Arriving there, I soon engaged in teaching in the colored schools again, and thanked God that in all the varied vicissitudes of war opportunities of usefulness were afforded me.

I remained in New Orleans until March of 1865,* at which time I became convinced that the difficulties which had prevailed in Mexico had become so much lessened as to justify me in taking up the line of march towards that long-desired post of usefulness. Accordingly, I took passage on a United States transport, and went to Brazos, as that port was still retained by the Federals. Remaining there one night I was conveyed in a Government ambulance to the opposite landing of Bagdad. A detail of soldiers accompanied us, as there was no safety, on account of the Confederates lying about in ambush. Several balls whistled by us. I crossed the Rio Grande, and found Bagdad greatly improved since the time which we could find no other accommodations there but the hold of a schooner. Business houses of all kinds had been erected, and its general appearance indicated it to be a first-class commercial town. Vast quantities of goods from all parts of the world had been passed through Bagdad, by which the whole South had been supplied.

---

* This was the time that Maximilian determined upon religious liberty in Mexico.

I went to the St. Charles Hotel, and found no difficulty in obtaining entertainment, until I could obtain conveyance to Matamoras. While I was there, news came of the surrender of General Lee's army, and I had the opportunity of witnessing the effects of that painful intelligence upon those who had staked their all upon the ultimate triumph of the Southern Confederacy.

Expressions like these were made:

" It can not be possible that our righteous cause can fail!" " Justice and right must and *will* prevail."

Another said:

" It is an act of strategy on the part of General Lee. He is feigning to evacuate Richmond, and going to withdraw his army to cut off Sherman and the whole host of Yankees."

" Do not fear! we shall see greater fighting than we have seen yet, and the South will surely come off victorious." This man seemed to be quite an oracle among them, and hope sprang up in all minds, that the news just received was all a hoax.

The great calamity it would prove to Bagdad if the war should end was also discussed. One man expressed his deep regret by saying:

" If this news be true, no more cotton and goods will be shipped through Bagdad."

Many like him would have been glad to have war and bloodshed continued indefinitely, if they could continue to make money.

As soon as convenient, I went on to Matamoras and looked for conveyance to Monterey, the place of my destination. While here, news arrived of the assassination of President Lincoln, and truly sad was the intelligence to many hearts. I was much gratified at the demonstrations made by the Confederate officer on the other side of the river. The commanding general forbade any expressions of disrespect towards the murdered president, under penalty of severe punishment. Some fellows, however, of the baser sort, did come over to Matamoras and hold a mock funeral, which act received the condemnation of Mexicans and Americans generally.

After waiting several days, a stage was announced to start for Momterey, if possible to get through the obstacles which obstructed the way. No less than three distinct governments were in existence. Matamoras was in possession of the Imperialists, Monterey of the Juarists, and about midway between the two Cortinas had established his government. I felt some concern about starting under such circumstances, but finally concluded to do so, and the morning of starting I said to a friend, " What do you think of my attempt to go to Monterey ? " He replied, " If it was any one but yourself, I should say it was extremely hazardous ; but *you* seem proof against disaster or accident." I started, and was favored in having an American gentleman for a fellow passenger, who very kindly rendered me all necessary assistance. Our driver, who was a Mexican, proved an expert in getting through the lines of the different governments, and after six days travel we arrived safely in Monterey. I was truly happy, after so many delays, to find myself in my long-desired field of labor.

CHAPTER XVI.

Seeking Protestant head-quarters—No missionary Society had
entered Mexico—The agent of the American Bible Society
scattering the Bible—Fruits apparent—Necessity of a permanent Protestant Mission—Monterey regarded the most
important point—Suitable buildings necessary—Resolve to
come to the United States for money —Trip from Monterey to Matamoras—Taken prisoner by Cortinas—Favor
found with robbers—Fate of other travelers—"Blue
Coats" pass unhurt.

MR. HICKEY had been scattering the Bible broad
cast over Northern Mexico for two years, and
precious fruit was apparent. There were already
many converts, and we had reason for believing
that much fruit was waiting to be gathered from
the seed already sown. My impressions were, that
the promising indications justified the permanent
establishment of a Protestant mission at some
point in Northern Mexico.

Monterey, on account of its commercial interests,
was the most important city of this portion of the
country, containing a population of about forty
thousand inhabitants. It was the center of strong
Roman Catholic influences, and whether to plant a
mission where Satan's seat seemed so strongly en-
trenched, was a vital question. Some persons who
were acquainted with the prejudices existing there,
advised me to seek a place less under Romish

power. But after mature deliberation, I came to the conclusion that as we must have error to compete with in any locality to which we might go, it was as well to attack the strongholds, and "grapple with the prince of darkness on his throne," by establishing the truth in the very heart of his dominions.

The weapons we designed to employ were of a caliber which justified our advance upon Satan's batteries, although glistening with his choicest artillery. Availing myself of all the information and counsel possible, after three months investigation, I decided to fix the head-quarters of Protestantism at Monterey. In order to secure all necessary advantages, I found we must have a building, over which we could exercise undisputed control. During the three months I had been in Monterey, I had rented three houses, and had to move as many times, for as soon as the priests found I was teaching the Bible, they always found means to dispossess me of the house. Protestant worship was kept up by the converts in their own houses; yet, I could see how greatly it would facilitate the cause, and give it repute, to have a suitable place for Divine worship. We needed, also, accommodations for schools, as I had found these auxiliaries indispensable to the prosperity of a Protestant mission. I resolved to come to the United States, which I was happy to know had ended its long night of war, and see if I could obtain aid for the

11

erection of suitable buildings for the contemplated mission.

I left Monterey in August of '65, and it may not be amiss to give some of the incidents of my journey by the way.

During my stay in Monterey the Imperialists had come into power. We retired one night the subjects of a Republic, and arose the next morning under the dominion of an Empire—the Republicans quietly evacuating during the night, and the Imperialists taking possession. Consequently, Monterey and Matamoras were now both under the same government; but Cortinas still maintained his reign in the intervening territory, much to the disquietude of the people, especially to that of travelers. His principal intention was to harass the Maximilian government by cutting off all communication by mail, and hindering the transfer of goods. But he was nowise scrupulous whom he encountered, provided booty could be obtained.

He had assumed the character of a regular guerrilla chieftain, having under his control about a thousand desperadoes of like character with himself. It had become extremely hazardous to travel through his dominions, and every stage attempting to pass met with portions of his command, and passengers were dispossessed of every thing they had, escaping only with their lives. There was no other way for me to get to the frontier but to pass these banditti, as they extended in all directions, so as entirely to intercept travel.

I waited some time for more favorable indications before I should feel justified in starting.   Finally, a train of merchandise arrived in Monterey from Matamoras, having been protected from Cortinas' grasp by a convoy of several hundred French soldiers, and although constantly beset, it had succeeded in getting through.   This convoy was to return to Matamoras, and it was thought stages might go along safely under its protection.   There were two lines of stages, the proprietor of one being an American; that of the other, a Mexican. The former immediately decided to go, and it was deemed prudent for some of the merchants to send along a considerable amount of specie—some one hundred thousand dollars or more.   One million was first proposed, but that amount was regarded quite too hazardous.

I was invited by the American to go in his stage. He said to me, "I mean to get through safely, and I will see that you do also."

Although advised to do so by other friends, I could not feel willing to go under the protection of French soldiers.   My impression was very strong that the French had no right to be in Mexico, and I felt that I could not ask God to protect me by means of these foreign aggressors.   Besides, I well knew that Cortinas would be informed of the valuable prize, and that no efforts would be lacking to secure such a booty. Bullets would, I doubted not, be flying from the ambush of the banditti, and I did not choose to put myself in the way of them.

I declined, from my own personal convictions, but several others, who had been waiting for conveyance, took passage and left Monterey. The day after the departure of this stage, the proprietor of the other line proposed starting, and going along without any convoy. I immediately concluded to go, for quite satisfactory reasons to my own mind. In the first place, we were requested to take no baggage, therefore we would offer no prize to Cortinas. Another weighty reason was that the driver was a Mexican, the same with whom I had traveled a few months before, and I already knew his powers of conciliation with his own people, and I had reason to believe that he would prove an expert in dealing with the ruffians we might have to encounter.

Several others concluded to go, among whom were two ladies—one a German, the other a Mexican. My friends furnished me with all needed supplies for any emergency; and one kind friend, who had made ample provision, as she said, for a sojourn in Cortinas' camp, remarked with much apparent sadness, "I should feel much better about you, if you had gone with the convoy."

At 4 P. M. of the second day after the departure of the other stage, we started, and, as we passed from the outskirts of the city, I felt conscious of a convoy accompanying us, but not of "French soldiers." All fear departed, and we traveled on without molestation until the close of the fifth day. Occasionally some one would say, "There are the robbers!" But if there, they did not molest us. We stopped, intending to remain a few hours, but were informed that the convoy had passed only three hours before. This was regarded a dangerous proximity, as we had no desire to share their chances of escaping Cortinas. Our driver immediately started on another road (as roads abound in Mexico) and we traveled all night, excepting a few hours for the mules to rest. In the morning we came to a ranch, and upon inquiry, found we were but a short distance from the camp of Cortinas! There was no retreat then, and it was thought much better to go forward than attempt to evade him, so we went bravely on. Soon we were met by a company of horsemen, who informed us we must go to the camp as prisoners. Arriving there, we were told that Cortinas was distant some ten miles, and he would have to be brought before any disposition could be made of us. Our carriage was driven into the center of a large space, around which were stationed vast numbers of armed men, some on foot and some on horses, evidently prepared for any emergency.

Our mules were removed, and we remained sitting in the stage. Looking about, I saw several men lying around on the grass evidently sick. The thought immediately struck me: I will try and alleviate their sufferings, and let these people see I am a friend to them, although their prisoner. Accordingly, I took some articles of food and choice delicacies, got out of the carriage, and walked very deliberately about among the sick. Finding some with a burning fever, I administered to them such cordials as I had. One asked for camphor, which I regretted, I could not give him. But I felt gratified in imparting even a ray of comfort to suffering humanity, although to such a rough class of human beings. I returned to the stage, and very soon it was surrounded by men who looked as if they too would like some token of my favor. I disposed of my ample supply of provisions among them, and found I was fast making friends in my new quarters. Knowing Mexican character so well, I was perfectly assured I had gained considerable ground in securing personal protection in any emergency in which I might be placed.

An officer, who seemed to have charge, rode up, and I asked him if I had any reason for apprehending danger? He seemed much mortified at my suggestion and replied, "An American lady shall not be harmed." In about five hours, Cortinas' approach was heralded by a band of martial music, and soon he, with his body-guard, was before us. He was the complete personification of a guerrilla chief. His Indian face and evil eye, portrayed the desperate character he had for many years sustained upon the frontier; and we felt any thing but comfortable while he sat on his horse in silent contemplation, evidently considering what he should do with us. My worst apprehensions were that he would take our carriage and mules, and leave us helpless in the midst of our journey.

After some time of suspense, Cortinas put his hand upon his stomach, and looking earnestly at us, said, "Yo tengo hambre," (I am hungry.) We immediately took the hint that he wanted his dinner, and we were not slow in bringing our best supplies for the occasion—sending them into a jacal near by. Cortinas and his staff went in, and, after remaining about half an hour, came out, looking very good natured, and, after some conversation with our driver, gave him a pass, and bade us go in peace.

I was informed, while in camp, that Cortinas was going out that night to attack the convoy and stage, and obtain the money, of which they were perfectly well informed. With such a prize in view we were let off as of comparatively small importance. I felt anxious for the passengers, some of whom I knew, but could do nothing for them, but lift a prayer to God that their lives might be spared.

On account of a quarantine at Brazos, I was detained at Brownsville some four weeks. Great apprehensions were felt for the other stage, and it was fully three weeks before any reliable information could be obtained of its fate. A courier, at length, arrived from Monterey bringing the news that Cortinas did really attack the convoy, killing and taking prisoners many of the soldiers, and robbing the stage of the money, but permitting the passengers to return to Monterey.

An ex-confederate general and his aid, who were traveling in their own carriage, were murdered, while four thousand dollars in gold, and their horse and carriage, were taken by Cortinas.

It was said at that time that a man with a "blue coat" could pass Cortinas' camp unhurt, while a "gray coat" would uniformly come up missing. The attitude which the United States government assumed in regard to expelling the French from Mexico, and also the designs of the South toward Mexico in case of the success of the Confederacy, were fully understood by the Mexican people. This explained the difference of treatment.

CHAPTER XVII.

Arrive in New York—The American and Foreign Christian
Union approve my plan—No money in their treasury for
building purposes—Obliged to make personal solicitation
from individuals—First donation $500—Other liberal con-
tributions—Crowning donation, $10,000, by one individual
—Obtained the necessary amount—Returned to Monterey—
Rev. Mr. Hickey's death—Mr. Thomas Westrup appointed
by the B. S. as successor—Purchased a building for the
Protestant mission—To be enlarged and remodeled—Mexican converts would make good missionaries—Decided to
employ four—Wrote to the A. & F. C. U. for the means—
No money could be granted—Resolve to go to the U. S.
and obtain it—Approved by the Board—Come to N. Y.—
Appeal to the Christian ladies—Favorable response by the
ladies of Hartford and New Haven, Conn.—Sufficient
means obtained for employing eight men from different
sources—Returned to Monterey—Mission house ready for
occupancy—Commissioned the Bible readers to go forth—
Success of their labors about Monterey.

AS soon as the quarantine was raised at Brazos, I
took the first steamer for New Orleans; and
from thence, came by sea to New York, arriving the
first of October. My plan of erecting a church and
school building in Monterey was approved by the
Board of the American and Foreign Christian
Union, but no aid from the society could be granted,
as there were no funds in the treasury for building
purposes. I was thrown upon the benevolence of

individuals, and again was obliged to make personal
solicitation. The proposition **to obtain** fifteen thou-
sand dollars, the amount which I felt the object **de-**
manded, was regarded by the board **as somewhat**
extravagant, **and** it was suggested by **some of the**
members that I should modify my expectations. As
exchange was at that **time,** fifteen thousand **in cur-**
rency was only equivalent to ten thousand in specie,
and, **I very well knew,** that **I could** not purchase
or build, **as property was estimated** in Monterey at
that time, an edifice **to answer all necessary purposes**
for any less sum than **ten thousand** dollars. I was
aware of an improved state of feeling of my **Amer-**
ican friends toward Mexico, and I fully believed **I**
should find persons who would contribute liberally.

I started out **on** the **arduous and trying labor,**
and was most agreeably surprised upon my first application to receive a **five** hundred dollar donation
from a merchant, T. N. Dale, Esq., of New York.
I continued **to realize liberal contributions from**
Christian **gentlemen, both in New York and Bos-**
ton. But my crowning donation was *ten thousand*
dollars from one individual, E. D. Goodrich, Esq.,
of Boston. This liberality was quite an advance **on**
what I received in my early solicitations for Mexi-
co. In former times I was satisfied and thankful
with a *"one dollar"* donation, and, *"* not having **de-**
spised the day of small things," the **Lord rewarded**
me by this remarkable display of his faithfulness
and loving kindness. "Be thou **faithful over a**

few things, and I will make thee ruler over many things."

In May of 1866, I had procured in money and pledges sufficient for my object; and again set my face toward Mexico, truly happy and thankful to my kind friends who had so generously aided me in my enterprise.

Upon my arrival in Mexico, I found a republic again, although in an unsettled condition. Juarez had returned to the capital, and law and order were being restored as far as possible, under the difficulties which abounded throughout the country.

I rented a house, opened a school, and began to look for a favorable location for building or purchasing one already built, and remodeling it, so as to answer all our demands. The distribution of the Bible was progressing with encouraging prospects, but in the midst of Mr. Hickey's useful labors, he was, in November, 1866, suddenly removed by death. More than a passing tribute is due this man for his unwearied labors to circulate the Word of Truth among the benighted people of Mexico. A valuable friend was lost to the cause of evangelical religion when this good man was called to lay off his armor for his rest on high. His name still lives among this people for whom he labored, and long will those hills and valleys which he traversed be bearing fruit from the precious seed he scattered. The American Bible Society appointed another agent, Mr. Thomas Westrup, who also had Mexican evangelization at heart, and the work continued to go on prosperously.

After some months looking, waiting, and counseling, I determined upon a location for planting the first Protestant mission in Northern Mexico, as far as mission premises were concerned. An edifice, occupying a very favorable position in the city, formerly built and owned by a Catholic priest, was for sale, and which seemed adapted to our demands. I availed myself of the advice of judicious persons who were interested in the mission, and their opinion corresponding with mine, finally brought me to the conclusion to make the purchase. The price I paid for the property was regarded by competent judges a very low figure for that time. The man of whom I purchased was offered the day after he sold to me, five hundred dollars in gold for the bargain; but this Mexican, to his honor, replied, "I have passed my word to the lady, and she shall have it."

Although the building was very well finished for a Mexican house, yet it required enlarging and remodeling to answer the triple office of chapel, schools, and residence. I was recommended to an Englishman, who was said to be a competent man, and engaged him, at a fair compensation, to do the work.* Several months would elapse before the building would be completed for occupancy, and I

---

* The contract was made and writings were drawn up by a competent business man, an American, and friend to the mission.

looked around to see what work might present it-self in the meantime.

Converts to the Protestant faith had multiplied; and some of the men, by continued and devoted study of the Scriptures, had become quite capa-ble of instructing their fellow-countrymen in those truths which they had found precious to their own souls. It occurred to me that a good working force might be made out of those Mexican converts, for propagating the Gospel in Mexico. Indeed, I be-lieved that they were better prepared for efficient service than any foreign missionaries who might be brought upon the field, who, of course, would be entirely unacquainted with the peculiarities of Mex-ican character and customs. Although unlearned in any of the sciences, except what they had learned from the Bible, I doubted not that they might be able to explain salvation by Christ, to the saving of many souls.

I then selected four of the converts, and asked them if they would be willing to go out among their people abroad and preach Christ.

They said they would like to do it, but they had their families to support by their daily labor, and, consequently, could not give their whole time.

I inquired the amount required for their families.

They said, "About thirty dollars a month."

I then put the question, "If I will provide for your families, will you give all your time to the spread of the Gospel?"

They answered in the affirmative, but wished it distinctly understood that they would not be *paid* for preaching the Gospel; for, said they, "that must be without money, and without price."

The matter being settled with them satisfactorily, I wrote to the American and Foreign Christian Union, asking for the means of putting these men into the field, which "was already white for the harvest." I received the reply that no money could be granted for the proposed work, as their treasury was already overdrawn for work in other lands. But could such a work as that presented to me be relinquished because of this refusal?

Must souls, for whom Christ died, be left to perish in Mexico for the want of money? Nay, verily, I will get it. He who has declared "the silver and the gold to be his," will surely unlock the hearts of his people to furnish the means, that His name may be glorified in the salvation of souls even in Mexico. So I took my life again in my hand, or rather put it into the hands of my long-tried Preserver, and performed another hazardous journey out of Mexico, arriving in New York in May, 1867.

My course was approved by the Society, and full permission was granted me for making independent solicitations for my object. I did not think proper to go to the churches, as most of them were already contributing to the Union, but decided to appeal to the Christian women of the land to aid in sending out these native teachers of the Gospel in Mexico.

Nor did my decision prove a vain speculation. While waiting in New York for Divine direction I received a letter from the ladies of Hartford, Conn., inviting me to come there and give some account of the work in Mexico. Regarding the invitation as a hopeful indication of God's providence, I hastened to comply. A meeting was called, and I found an appreciative audience. These Christian ladies took the measure of my purpose, heartily indorsing the plan, and came forward and pledged one thousand dollars annually for the support of native Bible-readers and colporteurs in Mexico. With letters of recommendation, I went to New Haven, Conn., and a similar meeting was called, and another thousand dollars pledged. Need I enlarge upon the emotions of gratitude which sprang up in my heart at this noble demonstration of woman's love for the work of her Divine Master? I felt like applying those precious words which our Saviour used in regard to the services of one of old: "Wheresover the gospel is preached throughout the whole world, this that these women have done shall be spoken of as a memorial of them." Truly, I thanked God and took courage, believing I should yet see the Gospel preached in Mexico *by the Mexican themselves.*

As the time for my return had not arrived, I concluded to continue my solicitation and obtain money for putting more native converts into the work, as I knew they might be found. I visited some other places in New England and in the State of New York, and from the Christian ladies I obtained, after a few months, sufficient funds for employing seven or eight men.

With exultant hopes, I returned and found my building ready for occupancy. In it we commenced public worship on the Sabbath, holding also two meetings a week; and I opened a school for Mexican girls. As soon as practicable, I gathered together my missionary band of native laborers, sending them out two and two, as our Saviour sent out the early disciples. This accorded with their views, as they believed the examples of Scripture to be their only guide. The Bible, distributed by the Society's agents, had prepared the way, and many souls were longing for more light and instruction.

The morning of their starting out upon the work, when they came for their instructions, I noticed two of the youngest men looked troubled, and I inquired the cause.

They said they were afraid they would meet with opposers, and that they might not be able to refute arguments which enemies might bring against the Bible; particularly they feared a priest whom they expected to encounter in the way.

I read to them the tenth chapter of Luke, in which is the account of Christ sending out the seventy, and drew their attention to the expression, "and he sent them two and two before his face into every city and place, *whither he himself would come*," particularly the last clause. I said to them, "You are going out in Christ's name to preach His Gospel, and you may expect His presence and blessing as he has promised." Their confidence seemed to be renewed, and they cheerfully took their bundle of books and departed.

Need I say this was an auspicious morning to me? As these messengers of a pure Gospel went forth to dispense light and truth in that dark papal land, my heart burst forth in joyful exclamations in behalf of Mexico: "Arise, shine; for thy light is come, and the glory of the Lord is risen upon thee."

At the close of the month they all returned, each with a favorable report. They had been kindly received and entertained for the valuable instructions they were able to impart. Those two young men who went forth trembling came back rejoicing, saying, "Every one whom we met listened to our teachings without any opposition; and even the priest whom we so much dreaded said no harm of the Bible."

I turned to the scene of the return of Christ's laborers and read of the seventy returning again with joy, saying, "Lord, even the devils are subject unto us through thy name."

Thus these men continued, from month to month, traversing the country within the circle of one hundred miles around Monterey, teaching and preaching the things concerning the kingdom of **God.** They went from house to house and from **ranch to** ranch, and many souls were brought out of **darkness** into the light and liberty of the Gospel.

CHAPTER XVIII.

FEELING we must penetrate "the regions beyond," I concluded to send two of the laborers
into the State of Zacatecas, a distance of some three
or four hundred miles. I selected the two young
men already mentioned, who, with two of the Bible Society's colporteurs, went forth dispensing the
Gospel on their entire route. Arriving at a place
called Villa de Cos, they remained for several
weeks, teaching and preaching with great success.
The State of Zacatecas had been highly favored by
the residence of an American, a decided Christian
gentleman, for some years, whose influence, no
doubt, had prepared the way somewhat for the remarkable fruits which resulted from the labors of
our native Bible-readers.

Perhaps I can not better present the aspect of

the work at that time than by inserting a letter published in the December number, 1868, of the "Christian World," organ of the A. & F. C. U. It was written by a gentleman occupying a distinguished political and social position, a resident of Zacatecas. The letter was dated Cos, July 4, 1868. He says:

"I believe that it will be satisfactory for you to know the development which the religious sentiment is undergoing in this country; and how true it is, as we have considered, that if evangelical ministers would come to labor here, the light of truth would rapidly spread abroad and diminish the influence of that fanaticism which the Romish clergy has established. In consequence of some sellers of Bibles and other religious books, having come here from Monterey, public attention has been awakened in a lively manner. . . . . . . Several persons interested by the simple *reading* of the Scriptures, united for the purpose of diligently studying them. At first, they were few, but have gradually increased, until, on the arrival of Mr. Westrup, Bible agent, about forty received baptism (by pouring), and partook of the communion, according to the Protestant sense of it, as a solemn memorial of the sacrifice of Christ.

"Did you anticipate any thing of this kind? Probably not; knowing as you do, the terrible influence of our clergy, who now, however are astonished at the wide breach that has been opened in their dominion. Behold then, how, at the first gleam of light over these regions, we discover that the soil is fertile, and only requires intelligent workmen to cultivate it in order to utterly cast down that sacerdotal rule which has occasioned such untold evils in this country, degrading and demoralizing its inhabitants."

Among the number who professed conversion, were two highly educated Mexican men—a father and son, who, upon the departure of our Bible-readers, took up the work and continued to carry it forward successfully. They soon started a periodical, called "The Evangelical Torch," a paper which circulated quite extensively, enlightening public sentiment generally, and valiantly defended the Truth against the most violent opposers. I take the liberty of continuing a brief history of this work in Zacatecas.

Two years after this work commenced, there was a membership of the church, of one hundred and seventy members, and an edifice had been erected, mainly by the Mexicans themselves. In 1871, an urgent request was made to the American and Foreign Christian Union for a foreign missionary. This Board could not furnish a man who could speak the Spanish, and the Presbyterian Board of Missions having a man who had labored in South America, whom they could put immediately into the field, it was thought best by the A. & F. C. U. to transfer the Mission to the Presbyterian Board; and since

November of 1871 * this mission has been under their auspices, and I am happy to know is receiving a good share of prosperity.

But to return to the mission of Monterey and its vicinity. Perhaps I can not better exhibit the aspect of the work, as it presented itself at that time, than to copy some of the letters I wrote, which were published in the " Christian World."

To a disinterested observer, I doubt not, my descriptions may appear somewhat embellished, but some degree of allowance may be made for my standpoint. Having looked upon Mexico years before, shut up in papal darkness, with scarcely a ray of hope, how could I feel otherwise than joyful and exultant at the manifest evidence of the power of truth over superstition and error?

Would the military soldier who had skirmished long upon the outskirts of the enemy's country, with scarcely any human hope of ever getting a foothold, feel otherwise than exultant when he plants himself in the heart of that land, and finds all barriers to his permanent occupancy gradually disappearing? I am sure not. But to the letters: The following is dated, Monterey, December, 1868:

" Not since the glorious days of Martin Luther, in which divine truth electrified the blinded subjects of the apostate church into a new life, has there been

---

* On account of a revolution in Mexico, missionaries were not sent until November, 1872.

a more remarkable exemplification of its potency than we are witnessing at the present time in Mexico. It is truly gratifying to see with what satisfaction these long deluded followers of Rome take the precious truths of God's Word into their inmost hearts.

"All ages and conditions are alike influenced by its transforming power. A man who had been a terror to the country around, by his savage conduct, has been so changed that he has the spirit of a lamb. His wife, who was often obliged to hide herself to escape his beatings, providentially met with a poor girl, who had become a convert to the truth, to whom she related the brutal treatment she frequently received from her husband. This girl told her of the religion which the Bible taught, in which husbands were commanded 'to love their wives and be not bitter against them.' The unfortunate woman was forcibly struck with the blessedness of such a religion, and begged the girl to get the book which contained it, and possibly she might prevail upon her husband to read it. The girl had no Bible herself, as she could not read, but had heard what she told the woman at the Protestant meeting.

"A Mexican woman, who was a Christian, was urged to come and read the Bible to her husband. And strange to say, the savage man listened with attention to this first knowledge he had ever received from God's Word. He became deeply interested, and after abandoning one sin after another, he has become entirely a changed man in heart and conduct. As soon as his mind began to be enlightened he tore down his images, with which his house abounded, and threw them away. His own language to one of our colporteurs soon after this great change, was: 'We have been taught to worship devils instead of God. The church of Rome is as different from the church of Christ, as hell is from heaven. How beautiful is the religion of Christ.'

"His wife also rejoices in the truth. It is now three months since his conversion, and he seems to be growing more and more sensible of the great sinfulness of his past life, and the great obligation he is under to God for snatching him 'as a brand from the burning.'

"Wherever our Bible-readers go, souls are brought into the kingdom. Two went, two weeks ago, to Montemoreles, a town of some thousands of souls. They write me, 'Never have we seen a people so desirous to hear the truth, as contained in the holy Scriptures. Scarcely can we get time to eat and sleep, so anxious are they to hear our readings in God's Word. Several have professed conversion, and given evidence that they are born again. Among the number is an aged woman of sixty-nine, and a boy of thirteen years. Two men who threatened to shoot the colporteurs if they came there with their Bibles, are now sitting at the feet of Jesus in their right minds.' That Mexico is ripe for the Gospel, facts in abundance plainly show. And that God is most wonderfully raising up native agencies to cultivate this promising field, is equally evident."

In connection with this letter, written 1868, I will insert an extract from the "Missionary Herald" (organ of the A. B. C. F. M.) of February, 1875, in which is made mention of the mission in Montemoreles. I desire to do this to show to my readers that this early work of native Bible-readers was not evanescent, but has proven by its fruits to be genuine Gospel work. But to the extract:

"In October (1874) Mr. Herrick again visited several out-stations. At Montemoreles seven persons were received to the church, three of them heads of families. Mr. Herrick says no other one of their churches is increasing in numbers so fast as that of Montemoreles, and he thinks the converts are of a worthy class."

In another letter of 1868 which I copy from the "Christian World," I said : "Although I wrote a short time ago, yet I trust another communication from me and Mexico will not come amiss. Incidents of an interesting character are taking place among us which I think can not fail to interest you. The Gospel has taken root in Mexico, and is producing fruits truly delightful. Never, in any land of papal darkness, has the Word of God shown itself to 'be sharper than a two-edged sword' with more certainty than in Mexico—a country where the 'mystery of iniquity' has so

13

long prevailed, and the 'wicked' one has so boldly revealed himself, 'even him whose coming has been after the working of Satan, with all power and lying wonders.' The people who have so long groaned under the oppressive yoke of that false system, are happy in finding a religion more tolerant in its demands.

"Those who have embraced the religion of the Bible acknowledge the freedom which the Truth has given them. I met, yesterday, with an old man of seventy years, who has recently been converted. His face beamed with happiness as I asked him: 'You find this new religion pleasant, do you?' He replied, 'Oh, yes, there is no yoke but is easy, and no burden but is light.'

"He came in from a small village, about forty miles from Monterey. He informed me that twelve persons, within a few months, had embraced the Gospel, and were rejoicing in it. Four of his own family, besides himself, were among the number. This work of grace was wrought through the instrumentality of a man, (Mexican), who was converted about a year ago in Cadereyta. Who can doubt that this man is called to preach Christ, when such fruits are manifest? I have never witnessed a work more truly evangelical, or seen more correct examples of true evangelists than we have among the Mexican converts.

"Last Sabbath there came into our Sunday-school two young men, who evidently, by their manner, came for the purpose of caviling, and turning our religion into ridicule. The superintendent met them at the door, asked them to take seats, and sat down by their side. After some little hesitation, one of them very impertinently inquired, 'What do you call yourselves? Methodists, Episcopalians, Baptists, or Presbyterians?' The superintendent very pleasantly replied, 'We call ourselves Christians.'

"The other visitor then inquired respecting our belief. He was answered by being shown the third chapter of John's Gospel, which he was requested to read. I observed his countenance changed while reading the solemn declarations of our Savior respecting the necessity of being 'born again,' in order to become a true Christian and fit for the kingdom of heaven. Immediately upon getting through they arose, saying, 'We will come again,' and politely withdrew. What struck me most forcibly was the *manner* in which their impertinence was met.

"Their appearance indicated that they belonged to the first class of society. They were no doubt champions of the Roman Catholic religion, but the simple truths of God's Word completely disarmed them, and I could readily account for the wonderful success which crowns the labors of these converted Mexicans. They present the truth as it is in Jesus, and it does not fail of its legitimate results. They find no better arguments than our

Savior's own most blessed words, and upon them they rely."

In another letter I say: " Our Bible-readers are traveling over these hills and mountains, teaching by the way-side, in the ranches, villages, and cities, wherever they can find people to hear them, and it is rare that they find the people otherwise than anxious to hear something about the new religion, of which they have already an indistinct account. Some express the greatest surprise that the Protestants teach such good things, as they had been told by the priests to avoid Protestant teachings more than murder or any other terrible crime.

" The spirit of controversy is scarcely found among them. Particular subjects, upon which they had relied for the support of their religion, are brought forward for explanation. For instance, a Bible reader was asked to explain how the words of Christ could be understood so as not to have it appear that *Peter* was the rock upon which the church was built. It was explained to the satisfaction of the inquirers that Christ was the chief corner-stone, and that he referred to himself, and not to Peter, when he said, ' Upon this rock will I build my church.' Six intelligent Mexicans were present, all of whom expressed the utmost gratification that this strong bulwark of the papacy was so easily removed. Does it not appear evident that the papal power sits loosely upon these people? The Mexicans have been steeped and dyed in the

Roman Catholic religion, and no longer than a dozen years ago Satan sat undisturbed upon his throne, with 'gates of brass,' and bars of iron, encompassing the miserable subjects of his kingdom.

"But lo! God's Word found its way into these dark regions, and revealed to these priest-bound people that human law had no right to enslave the consciences of God's accountable creatures. These long enslaved subjects of papal dominion arose *en masse*, and, after years of desperate struggle, obtained religious freedom. Satan's kingdom now totters, never again to be re-established in Mexico.

"Efforts have been made to restore again the supremacy of the Romish religion; but foreign bayonets and imperial power proved inadequate before the purpose of a determined people. The principles of religious freedom have taken such firm hold of the Mexican people, that no papal shackles can ever again enslave them. As well may the elements be stayed by human efforts, as the progress of truth be resisted when it gets firmly fixed in the mind. The Word of God can not be bound, and will not be, until Mexico is brought to know its truths in all their saving power. May the Lord hasten it in his own good time."

A subsequent letter shows some of the annoyances to which we were subject at this period, proving that *somebody* was getting his toes stepped on. The letter says:

"Rome, every now and then, gets much disturbed, and does all in her power to overthrow the religion of the Bible in Mexico. She has had several severe throes in Monterey since this building has been devoted to Protestant worship. During the bishop's recent visit, every means were used to disturb our worship, and had we occupied premises of which we could have been dispossessed, we should have been, in all probability, driven out. But we sat securely "under our own vine and fig tree," and let Satan roar without, until he apparently came to the conclusion that we could not be moved, and finally ceased his clamor.

"Romanism still lives in Mexico, but seems to have lost much of her subtilty, for in her attempts to oppose Truth she often defeats her own ill designs. About two months ago, two of our Bible readers entered the city of Durango, with their Bibles and other printed truth. The priests stirred up the populace against them to such a degree that their lives were in imminent danger. The order from these spiritual overseers was, 'Stop these heretical teachings or do away with the men.' Undaunted by their threats, our men appealed to the authorities, and a guard of soldiers was immediately sent to their protection, and they continued their teachings to numbers of people desirous of learning the truth. The Alcalde told them 'to preach to their heart's content, and if a regiment of soldiers was necessary for their safety, it should be granted.'

" Popery is evidently shorn of its most potent element—the power of coercion—and its former glory has in a great measure departed. In proportion as a pure Christianity is propagated, in the same ratio its hold on the hearts of the people becomes relaxed.

"As the strongholds of that apostate church are being broken down, 'the leaves which are for the healing of the nations,' are especially needed. The American Tract Society's publications are in great demand ; the *printed* truth, scattered broadcast over the country in the wake of the Bible, is now imperatively required. God has most wonderfully raised up agencies on the field for scattering the seeds of Divine Truth, and 'the wilderness and the solitary place' are being made glad by the heralds of the Gospel, who are being sent out to proclaim its truths.

" With due self-distrust and humility, they seem fully aware of their utter inability to do any good of themselves. Their dependence is upon their Divine Master, who, they confidently believe, calls them forth in his work. I trust the Christian ladies who have so nobly undertaken the support of these heralds of the cross, will not fail nor be discouraged until truth is established in this dark land."

CHAPTER XIX.

Mission commenced in the City of Mexico—Bibles had been
circulated by the British Bible Society—Rev. Henry C.
Riley sent by the A. & F. C. U.—His view of the work,
and success—Letter from an Englishman—Fields white
for the harvest.

NOT only had I occasion for rejoicing over the
promising aspect of the work in Northern
Mexico, but from other parts of the country came
cheering tidings. In 1869, Rev. Henry C. Riley
was sent by the American and Foreign Christian
to the City of Mexico. Mr. Riley had spent much
of his life in South America, consequently was well
acquainted with the Spanish language, and also of
Spanish character; besides, was a Christian gentleman eminently qualified to inaugurate and direct a
Protestant mission in this important field. Mr. R.
had, for some time previous, ministered to a church
in New York city composed of Spanish speaking
people. In the summer of 1868, I was in New
York, and met Mr. Riley, who had long been a
personal friend. Our meeting was in the Bible
House, and after the usual salutations, he said to
me, " Miss Rankin, why do you not go to the *City*
of Mexico, where there are two hundred thousand
souls, instead of laboring in Monterey of only about

forty thousand?" I replied that I felt I was in the field to which God's providence had called me; besides I thought forty thousand souls a goodly number to labor for. I then put the question, "Mr. Riley, why do *you* not go to the City of Mexico?" "Oh," said he, "I can not leave my Spanish church in New York; only yesterday a Cuban lady really wept because she had heard a report that I was going to leave." "How large a church and congregation have you?" "About two or three hundred." "But, Mr. Riley, can you feel justified in remaining here and preaching to a few hundred people who are surrounded with Gospel privileges, when you might go to the City of Mexico where there are two hundred thousand souls without *one* Gospel preacher?" Mr. R. cast his eyes toward the floor, and stood without speaking for several minutes; then looking up with a cheerful face, said, "Miss Rankin, I *will go*. Next August you will hear from me in the City of Mexico." We parted; and sure enough, I heard from Mr. Riley, at the proposed time, from the City of Mexico, and now let us hear what he says of his new field of labor. I quote:

"There is a perfect hurricane of Protestant feeling raging against the Roman church. I feel much as if I had suddenly found myself in the time of the Reformation. The great thing for us to do is to plant Christian churches and institutions here as rapidly as possible.

"Long have these native Christians looked to

their brethren in the United States in hope. May they now have their hopes realized. If the American Church will make an effort worthy of the opportunity Christ has given them in this land, Mexico might write one of the brightest and most deeply interesting pages in missionary history in the course of the next few years." *

This view of Mr. Riley, I believe, was not ungrounded enthusiasm, but the result of impressions suggested by the actual manifestations of the field. It appeared fully evident that the Holy Spirit was brooding over that whole land, and that only the proper means need be used for Him to descend with all his healing power into the hearts of multitudes of Mexican people, who had become utterly disgusted with the religion of Rome, and were waiting for a religion better adapted to the wants of their immortal natures.

To show that others saw things highly encouraging, I will copy a letter written to the "Christian World" by an English gentleman, who had been for many years a resident of Mexico. As some of the representations made by Mr. Riley and myself have been regarded as somewhat "rose-colored," I hope that the opinions of this staid Englishman may serve to remove the imputation and corroborate our statements of the circumstances of these needy,

---

* In two years after Mr. R. went to Mexico he had a church in the city of 400 members, and this mission became really the most important in the whole country, and continues to be so.

waiting people. This letter was dated, City of **Mexico**, May 17, 1869. **It** says:

"It is impossible to look at the present state of this country, (Mexico) without being sensible that now is the appointed **time for** every servant **of the most high—for every believer** in the blessed Savior **—for every** Christian **to** exert himself to the utmost **to assist these** unhappy people, who are now ready and *anxious* to receive the glad tidings of the Gospel. If the Christian brethren of the United States could see what I see, and feel what I feel, when I attend the meetings of the evangelical brethren; **if** they could see the more than **two hundred persons** united in **supplicating God, in reading and** hearing the Gospel, in singing **the expressive and** beautiful hymns with a manfully intense feeling of devotion, **they** would be convinced that there is no country which requires or deserves their assisstance more than this. Much has already been attained by the efforts **of some** earnest laborers **in** the good **cause.**"

* * * * * * *

The arrival **of** Rev. H. C. **Riley has** given **a** further stimulus to these laborers in the vineyard, since he has shown us how to direct **our** efforts, and **by teaching the** children **to sing, has** perfected **our** mode **of** worship, and **nearly doubled our con-** gregation.

"There **are** already **five or six** congregations which are calling loudly for aid—either for preachers or books. The former is very difficult to pro-

cure, and the latter are required by thousands. . .
After reading one, they beg more earnestly for more.
They see the Bible quoted in them, and their curi-
osity is excited, and their consciences are awakened.
They inquire, 'Can these things be so?' They get
the Bible to examine."

"Consider a population of eight millions of souls
to be saved—nearly all willing, and thousands anxious to learn the way to eternal life, which they will
by reading these books, and thus be led to the study
of the Scriptures. It is impossible for me to find
words to express the profound conviction which I
feel, that now is the appointed time to introduce the
true worship."

"Laborers, artisans, and even soldiers attend our
meetings. They are poor, and, therefore, more
willing to turn to Christ; are unlearned, but learn
all that is necessary for salvation in the Bible, and
the tracts which assist in understanding it. May
our Heavenly Father incline your hearts to help us."

CHAPTER XX.

IT was quite common for Mexicans, at this
period, after obtaining some knowledge of the
Bible to organize "Societies" for the purpose of
mutual instruction. The feeling seemed to prevail
that something must be done as a manifestation of
their utter disaffection toward the Church of Rome,
and as an earnest expression of desire for something better.

I will insert an article which was published at
that time, styled "An Invitation." It was dated

"OAXACA, *May* 24, 1868.

"SIRS:

"Jesus Christ, in establishing his religion, had
for his object the moralization of mankind, and we
know how much civilization has already advanced
in consequence of the promulgation of His doc-

trines, both in Europe and America. But in Mexico our conquerors brought us Catholicism—that is, the **doctrine of Jesus Christ** disfigured—fitted rather to brutalize than to moralize and civilize. Now, that beautiful system of **free examination is** presented to us—a system which so well harmonizes with the democracy that rules us—the doctrines of Jesus Christ should be at once adopted without any mixture or interpretation, but pure **as** they came forth from His Divine lips. We ought to do this, because we see that the nations that have done this are those in the **vanguard** of civilization, England in Europe, and the United States in America.

"Look at our country! What has Catholicism done for us? Transformed the greater part of **our people** into fanatics, ignorant and foolish, and **the** rest into indifferent philosophers. . . . Therefore **every** Mexican who desires the good of his country should labor by every means within his reach that every **shadow of** retrogression disappear.

"In order to obtain it, and that all this may not be purely visionary, it is necessary to establish a society which has for its object to instruct us in the doctrine of Jesus Christ; having its meetings on the **Sabbath;** and its secretary to open communication with other societies of this kind.

"This society, once established, liberty of worship in Oaxaca will be a reality, and, without doubt, if we are firm, consistent, and self-denying, our people will progress."

Another similar Society was formed in Saltillo, capital of Cohahuila, neighboring state of Nuevo Leon, called the "Society of Artezaus," showing the *first* steps of this great movement toward a pure Christianity. Its operations had frequently come to my notice through the Bible Society's agent, who had sometimes addressed them at their meetings. Three or four years after I went to Monterey, I received a letter, signed by twenty men, expressing the desire that I should send an evangelical minister to instruct them in their duty; also, asking for some books treating particularly upon the Bible. They gave me quite an elaborate description of their origin and design.

Their breaking away from the Church of Rome, it seemed, occurred several years prior to the proclamation of religious liberty in Mexico, and was produced by the reading of a Bible procured from a German Protestant (the same man whom I had supplied in 1857 and '58), and had their meetings secretly until liberty of conscience was granted, after which their operations were public. They had established and supported several schools, from which the Catholic catechism was excluded and the Bible was substituted.

I complied with their request for books, but could not send them a minister. I regret to state that Saltillo has never been permanently occupied by a Protestant missionary *—thus far, no suitable man could be obtained. Many things conspire to render Saltillo a highly important missionary cen-

---

* Rev. Mr. Park, an independent missionary, went there in 1869, but staid only a short time.

ter, and I hope it may soon become the scat of powerful Protestant influences through the agency of some missionary Board.

In 1869 I became convinced that our converts in and about Monterey should become properly organized into churches. Hitherto, congregations had been collected for worship, and men had been chosen and set apart for administering the sacraments. Rev. Mr. Hickey, the second Bible agent in Northern Mexico, administered the first baptisms by immersion, as that mode corresponded with the belief of the "Plymouth Brethren," of whose Society he was a member. After his death, his successor, Mr. Thomas Westrup, baptized converts both by immersion and by pouring water upon the head. At Villa de Cos, forty were baptized by the latter mode by Mr. Westrup.

In the early part of '69 I was obliged to come to the United States to procure funds for the mission, and before leaving I asked Mr. Westrup, who was then agent of the Bible Society, if he would draw up a "Confession of Faith," embracing the main articles of belief of our Mexican converts, remarking that I was frequently inquired of respecting their doctrines, and I wished for something to show which might satisfy the inquirers.

I added, also, I wished it more particularly on his (Mr. Westrup's) account, as I knew the Bible Society felt somewhat apprehensive that he might be introducing something of a denominational character to his labors; his duty being, according to established rules, the distribution of the Bible, without note or comment. Mr. Westrup very willingly acceded to my request, and drew up a confession of faith, to which he said, "every Mexican convert would subscribe," admitting *three* modes of baptism, sprinkling, immersion, and pouring, stating most emphatically that "importance was not attached to the *mode*."

I was satisfied with the document, and brought it on to New York, showing it to the American and Foreign Christian Union, and to the Bible Society, and entire satisfaction was expressed by the officers of those Boards.

I had been in New York about two months when I received a letter from Mr. Westrup, stating that he was under the necessity of informing me that he had changed his mind since my departure upon the subject of baptism. He said, he and all the converts had decided to become Baptists, and that "henceforth the Mexican churches would practice immersion only, and commune only with those who were thus baptized." I immediately wrote a reply, that "my object had been to bring souls to Christ in Mexico, and that, in the choice of their mode of baptism, I had no dictation to make." As a missionary of the American and Foreign Christian *Union*, I had not the right of opposing a Baptist church being formed of the Mexican converts. I closed my letter by saying, "I commit the important

14

matter to the Great Head of the Church." There I left it, feeling no particular anxiety about the matter, if souls could only be saved, and continued my work of collecting funds for the mission. Sometimes the thought occurred, "Why should I labor to bring souls to Christ with whom I can not be permitted to commune at *His* table?"

But my prevailing impression was, that Mr. Westrup was laboring under a very great misapprehension in regard to the sentiments of our Mexican Christians. Although there were some who preferred immersion, yet I well knew they had by voluntary and united consent, entirely abandoned the doctrine of close communion, which Mr. Hickey had instituted. After we occupied the mission house, the communion was open to all who loved our Lord Jesus Christ. I could not believe that they would consent to be trammeled again. Their idea was that they had always been subjected to *forms* in the Romish church, and they utterly rejected any thing that savored of exclusiveness or uncharitableness. Their great desire, I knew, was to profess Christ in a manner which would bring them into fellowship with all His true people.

In my communications to Monterey, I made no allusion to the subject, merely giving instructions to my colporteurs and teachers, and the work went on as usual. After some three months, I received a letter from the person whom I had left in charge there, inquiring, "Why do you not say something about the Baptist question, as I know you are acquainted with the facts, because Mr. Westrup read your letter to him about it before the congregation. Many of the native Christians said, 'The letter is beautiful, and that you had done more to bring the Gospel among them than any *man* had done.' They come every day, inquiring when you are coming back. But you need not hasten until you complete your business, as nearly all the converts stand firm upon the old platform. Don Brigido* has maintained his post under the greatest pressure of Mr. W. Some three or four in Monterey, and about the same number in Cadereyta have decided to go with Mr. Westrup and become Baptist." After the receipt of this information, I concluded that, as the Mexicans had decided the matter themselves, I would take hold and aid them by all proper and Christian means, in the organization of churches, in which, I felt assured, the great majority of the members would unite in *one* communion.

When I returned to Monterey, I was happy, the day after my arrival, in meeting the beloved native Christians, and finding a uniform sentiment prevailing, except with a very few, who preferred attaching themselves to Mr. Westrup.

I very soon procured an evangelical minister, Rev. John Beveridge, who had labored for several years in South America, and he immediately organized churches in Monterey, San Francisco, and Mes-

* Our principal native preacher.

quital.   At Cadereyta an evangelical church had
been previously organized by Rev. Mr. Parke,* an
independent missionary, so we had *four* churches
which were in sympathy, and co-operated together
in harmony.   The dissensions seemed to be fast
healing, when Mr. Westrup decided to resign his
connection with the Bible Society, with a view of
accepting an appointment from a Baptist Board of
Missions of New York for laboring in Monterey.

I have ascertained through the secretaries of this
Board, that they had received information (though
not by any one on the ground) that there were Baptists among the converted Mexicans at Monterey.
Also, that they had written to Mr. Thomas Westrup,
making inquiries, and if such was the case, offering
to assume the support of the mission, placing him
at the head of it.   These facts account for the sudden change of Mr. W.'s sentiments.

I feel perfectly confident that if the Baptist
brethren of New York had understood matters as
they really existed and proved themselves afterward,
they would not have done what they did, in sowing
discord among these newly-converted members of
the Mexican mission.   These "babes in Christ,"
were utterly unprepared to understand denominational issues, being totally at a loss to comprehend
how disunion could possibly exist among Christ's
true followers.

---

* I afterward employed Mr. Parke to labor with us, and he
remained in our employ about two years.

Mr. Westrup went on to New York, resigned his agency of the Bible Society, received ordination and a commission from the Baptist Home Missionary Society, and in the August of 1870 returned to Monterey, and commenced most vigorously the work of breaking up all our churches and forming Baptist churches. For several months we were in constant turmoil, as Mr. W. and his followers were visiting our members at their homes, and in every possible manner trying to induce them to join the Baptists, telling them, as we were creditably informed, we "were no better than the Romanists, as we rejected the express commands of Christ."

It can easily be imagined that this state of things among Protestants was a great source of exultation among the priests, and for a few months we were struggling with difficulties with which our persecution from Romanists would bear no comparison.

During that time, however, we had several accessions to our communion, not only in Monterey, but in other places. Our churches were termed "Evangelical," as that term corresponded with the Mexican idea of gospel church. Mr. W. organized a Baptist church in Monterey, and in some other places succeeded in making proselytes.*

Two additional churches were soon added to our number, and we found it necessary to ordain some

* I have recently been informed that the Baptist Society of N. Y. has withdrawn its support, and Mr. Westrup has gone to Texas.

of our natives, who had already become quite acceptable preachers, so they might be properly qualified to administer the sacraments, and take entire charge of churches. Accordingly, two received ordination, and were sent to their respective fields. Six churches were already in successful operation, and more than that number of Protestant schools were planted in various places, besides a girl's and boys school in the mission building in Monterey. For these latter schools I was obliged to employ foreign teachers; but for the others I employed natives, who, although possessing a limited knowledge of the sciences, were quite competent to instruct their pupils in the knowledge of the Holy Scriptures.

A letter which I wrote about this time, published in the "Christian World," will probably give a better view of the situation and work than I am able to give at the present time. It says:

"We have abundant proof of the protecting care and spiritual benediction of the Great Head of the church in the events of the past year. I fully believe this Mexican mission will never have to pass a more severe ordeal; and as it has passed through unscathed, we have reason for hoping that its future progress will be more than ever before brilliant and successful. God has been better to us than our fears. Never has there been a time when our congregations were more influenced by the Word of Truth than during the past few months.

Many souls have let go their grasp of Romanism, and embraced the true gospel of salvation.

"We have in Monterey, at the present time, ten who are under examination, and will probably be baptized at our next communion. Also, in other churches there are hopeful subjects who are expressing the desire to become united with the people of God. We endeavor to be careful in admitting members, and receive none into communion until we have evidence that they are truly 'born again.' . . .

"The coming year must witness an enlarged plan of operations in this long-neglected country. We are endeavoring to open several new missions within a hundred miles of Monterey, and have already sent men to prepare the way by circulating evangelical reading, collecting congregations, and planting Sunday and week-day schools. The schools we find to be great auxiliaries, as through them the Bible can be introduced. The means for the support of our schools have been furnished by Sabbath-schools and Young Ladies' Institutions of the United States. . . . Our native evangelists and colporteurs have received, too, their entire support from the ladies abroad, and I trust their interest will not wane. These noble Christian women came to the rescue at a time when general indifference and even repugnance prevailed against Mexico and Mexicans, and I feel confident they will not desert the cause while the Savior is giving such evident testimony of His approbation of their liberality in behalf of souls for whom He died."

In a letter in June of 1870 I say:

" As the churches can be properly cared for in this vicinity, I have recalled four men to go into the States of Zacatecas, Durango, and San Luis Potosi, a distance of four hundred miles, and am just starting them off with Bibles and other books. My design is to open new fields in the regions beyond, and I wish I had the *means* of sending out *twenty* men instead of *four*. The fields are white for the harvest, and pleading for laborers. My spirit has no rest in view of the great work which might immediately be done in Mexico. . . . . Although we have had trials during the past year, the work has progressed, and at no previous time has it appeared more interesting and encouraging than at the present."

A highly interesting case came before us some little time later, affording another illustration of the power of the Bible, without any human agency. Agua Leguas, a place about one hundred miles from Monterey, was situated quite remote from any of the public thoroughfares, and had never, as any one knew, been visited by any of the agents or colporteurs. In the summer of 1871 one of our colporteurs, being in that portion of country, thought he would go to Agua Leguas and see if any thing could be done there. He went, and, much to his surprise, found quite a Protestant community, or, at least, several families, who had, for quite a length of time, congregated together for the purpose of studying the Scriptures. Our colporteur returned and reported the facts. Don Brigido Supulveda, our native minister, accompanied by a lay brother, went to examine and aid this little band of Bible-readers in their search after truth. These brethren remained some time, and found twelve who gave satisfactory evidence of having received the truth in the love of it. With instructions from Mr. Beveridge, a church was organized of believing Mexicans, whose sole instruction had been derived from the Bible and one other book, an exposition of Romanism, called "Nights with the Romanists," one of the Tract Society's publications. It seemed these books had come into their hands by some means, and the people, not being subject to the control of the priests, were free to investigate for themselves, and their conclusions were, that the system of Roman Catholicism, as portrayed by the "Nights with the Romanists," was false, and that the religion of the Bible, as they learned it in that book, was the only true religion. This church in Agua Leguas proved to be one of our staunchest churches; and who knows but there may be many other oases of a similar character in this great moral desert! Thousands of Bibles have been scattered by agents over that land, and we know not what silent work they may be accomplishing through the agency of God's Holy Spirit!

15

CHAPTER XXI.

Image of the Virgin destroyed—Protestants suspected—Dangers, seen and unseen—"Death to the Protestants" determined by a mob—A colored friend—Appeal to the Mexican authorities; also to the American Minister—Protection obtained—Destroyers of the image unknown—Supposed to be instigated by the priests—Persecutions overruled for the good of the mission.

DURING the winter of '69 and '70 we suffered much annoyance from the Romanists. On the 14th of December, the night before special devotions commenced to the Virgin Mary, an image of the Virgin, which was situated in a conspicuous part of the city of Monterey, was thrown down and broken to pieces. The destruction of this object, which had long been regarded with sacred devotion, of course produced a most profound sensation among the blinded devotees. The morning after the event, violent demonstrations were made towards the mission-house. Persons would pass and throw stones at the doors and windows, with various other insults. We were not aware of the cause, not having heard of the destruction of the image; and knowing it to be a "saint's day," we supposed the demonstrations to be merely an ebullition of their piety, which had been frequently exhibited on such occasions. Our schools continued their operations, and all our work went on as usual, although stones frequently came against our windows, breaking the glass. Late in the afternoon a multitude of men and boys gathered in front of the house, throwing stones, and also uttering threatening language.

Through a neighboring boy I learned that the image of the Virgin had been destroyed, and that the Protestants were suspected of being the cause. I was convinced, upon this information, that we were in serious danger, and sent immediately to the police head-quarters. After some time, several policemen came and dispersed the mob, arresting some whom they were able to capture, and sent them to jail : yet squads remained around, hidden from the authorities, and still continued their outrages as they could find opportunity. A guard was placed around the house; but I had but little confidence in the police, since they personally, as I had learned, were filled with indignation against the Protestants. At a late hour of the night I went to the door, and found one of the police sitting on the door-step, with his head bowed down, apparently asleep. I spoke to him, and, as I did so, a man came from the governor's house, across the street, and said to me in English, "Do not place any confidence in these men, for they shut their eyes so as not to see what is being done. I have heard them talk, and they are not friends to you."

I asked him who he was.

He said he was a colored man from Kentucky,

who had come to Mexico and joined the army, and was stationed at the bishop's palace (a military post near town); that he had been detailed that night as sentinel at the governor's house. "But," added he, "I will keep my eye on your house, and if I see any thing which might endanger you, I will give you warning, or notify the alcalda."

I thanked him—retired and slept a little.

Next morning several friends called—some advising us to leave the country immediately, as our lives were in imminent danger; saying that during the past night a quantity of gunpowder had been procured for blowing up the building; that parties were detected in injecting powder into the gutters under the building. Whether this was really true or not, I felt that I had some reason for fearing that something of the kind might be done. I did not, however, get my own consent to quit the field, but decided to remain and establish my legal right.

With a gentleman friend, a Frenchman, I went to the house of the alcalda (mayor of the city), and asked him if Americans were entitled to protection in Mexico.

"Why not?" said he. "*Certainly*, Americans are entitled to equal rights and privileges with Mexicans."

I then related to him my grievances, of which he was already apprised to some extent. He expressed the deepest regret, and said no efforts should be lacking on his part to suppress any further outrages. Notwithstanding the utmost vigilance of the authorities, daily outrages would be committed against the mission building, showing that public sentiment was not appeased for the loss of their dearly cherished idol.

"Death to the Protestants" was written in large letters occupying every available spot on the outside of the house. As the building was of stone, and no external combustible material, I had no cause of apprehending it might be set on fire, but I could not avoid having serious apprehensions that an effort might be made to destroy it with gunpowder. Our Mexican converts sympathized deeply in my grievances, and, for several weeks, one or two kept watch in and around the premises night and day.

I wrote, immediately after the disturbance commenced, to Mr. Nelson, United States Minister at the City of Mexico, but on account of a revolution prevailing in the vicinity of the capital, I did not get an answer for six weeks; but when the letter came, it was all I could desire. Mr. Nelson expressed the kindest sympathy, and said I should be protected in my peaceful mission, and gave me directions for procuring from the governor of the State an official guarantee for full and complete protection for the future. In case my presentation failed to receive proper attention, I was to inform him, and he would lay the matter before the general government at the capital.

I followed his directions, and, as soon as possible, papers were made out, signed by proper authorities, which secured to me and all my interests complete protection.

The authors of the destruction of the image have never been ascertained. I do not believe any of the Protestants were accessory to it, although the populace were made to believe it. Many believed that the priests instigated the whole affair for the purpose of raising a storm of persecution against us, so we should be compelled to leave the country, if not put to death by the mob. I was told by a reliable American gentleman, who was himself a Roman Catholic, that when the bishop visited Monterey during that year, he censured the priests greatly for permitting the Protestants to make such headway directly under their ministrations, and told them that if they did not go to studying and preaching in good earnest, and keep their people away from Protestant meetings, he would depose them. Whether the priests thought it would be easier to blow us up than to preach us down, "*deponent saith not.*" Our persecutions ceased, and nothing of a like serious nature has since occurred.

CHAPTER XXII.

Revolution of 1871—Commenced in Monterey—Dissatisfaction
with Juarez—Difficulty of obtaining soldiers—Bible-readers sought after—Colporteur work greatly hindered—Peace-
loving Mexicans—Mexicans supplied with arms—Battles
fought—Troops sent by Government—Great consternation
in Monterey—Battle fought six miles from the city—The
generals flee, and the soldiers rush into town to rob and
murder—Houses built like forts—Determine to protect the
mission property—Soldiers at the door and window, de-
manding life or money—Conciliate them with some refreshments—Four men killed on my sidewalk—Escape to
friends—Men brought to order.

IT becomes my sad duty to rehearse another case
of poor Mexico's scourge and disgrace—*revolution.*

Oh, why have not the turbulent waters of strife
been assuaged by the healing influences of the gospel of peace in Mexico? Ah, human nature is still
rife in Mexico as elsewhere! Ambition and political jealousy will never cease to rule poor fallen humanity until the brighter day of millennial peace
and glory.

In the autumn of 1871 a revolution commenced,
mainly inaugurated by General Treviño, governor
of Nuevo Leon, the State of which Monterey is the
capital, and assumed quite formidable proportions.
A dissatisfaction arose at the previous election of

Juarez—a party alleging that he had secured his election by fraud, and seeming determined to overthrow him and place another man in the presidential chair. Perfirio Diaz permitted himself to be proclaimed as the prospective president of the republic, and took the field himself. The feeling was quite prevalent that Juarez was assuming somewhat the character of a dictator; and having been in the presidency fourteen years, it was quite generally believed that a change would conduce to the good of the country.

As Mexicans are famous for an expression of feeling by words, it was inferred that union of effort would not be wanting for the overthrow of Juarez. But when the matter was fully tested, it was found that but two or three States would engage in actual combat. Nuevo Leon was the most conspicuous of these on account of some particular grievances which was conceived Juarez had imposed upon the people, and consequently was regarded by the government as the head-quarters of the rebellion. Consequently, Monterey being subject to an attack from the government at any time, was in a peculiarly dangerous condition. The winter of '71 and '72 was full of disquiet, as we were in constant apprehension of assault, and also our work was much disturbed by the effort to procure men for military purposes. Our colporteurs, teachers, and in some instances our preachers, were sought after to be pressed into service. Although our ordained ministers were **exempt** from military duty by the laws **of** Mexico, **yet they** were often sought after, and their congregations were very much lessened **because the male** members were obliged to hide themselves to avoid being compelled **to enter** the **army. A** general stampede **of** hundreds of Mexicans, **to** the mountains, greatly disturbed all kinds of business. **Heavy** prestimos (forced loans), **for military** purposes, were constantly made upon the merchants and **on all** who could pay any amount. I was obliged **to** meet the demand, **un**-der the threat of the confiscation **of the mission** property.

Judging **by the utter** dissatisfaction expressed by the majority **of the Mexican people under** these **rigorous** demands, **I should say there was** not a **people** under the sun who were more averse to war **than** these same poor Mexicans, whom **every** body **believes to** be ready to go into war merely from the **love** of it. **With** no patriotism **to inspire them,** they **would hide** themselves, **and the leaders of the** Revolution had to resort to every **kind of** strategy **to obtain a** sufficient number of men **to make any degree of show. My impressions are that it is** quite a small **portion of the population which pro**-**cures for the country the reputation it has. This** element is made up **mostly of Indian character, and** when no cause for revolution exists, these outlaws are engaged in guerrilla adventures for **purposes of robbery.**

Formerly, revolutions would be carried on without much loss of life, as their weapons consisted of old gun stocks, comparatively harmless, so that the combatants generally all came out alive, ready for another revolution when an opportunity was presented.

But since the French intervention, and our civil war, arms of an improved quality have been furnished, and battles have been quite sanguinary—thousands sometimes being left dead upon the field. Whether this is an improved condition of things, I hesitate to say, but one thing is evident: the discordant element of society in Mexico is becoming lessened by these bloody skirmishes, and perhaps after a few more years this faction may become so much decreased that the peace-loving party will predominate, and civil war and revolution cease to be the scourge and disgrace of that fair land.

Several bloody battles were fought during the winter within a hundred miles of Monterey, and in the interior Diaz carried on an unsuccessful campaign; being at last defeated, and obliged to flee to the mountains, where he soon died from disease. The revolutionary party still continued their efforts, after all hope of successful issue could possibly be entertained.

In the month of May it was announced that Government troops were approaching Monterey; of course, great consternation prevailed. Every available man was pressed into service, either to aid in the construction of fortifications, or to take the field. Heavy prestimos were demanded; some of the leading merchants refused to meet the demand from utter inability to furnish the money. In that case, they were forced to work on the fortifications; and a Spaniard, who formerly was a Spanish Consul, actually dropped down, completely overcome by the attempt to labor under the scorching sun. His friends carried him home, and by a compromise—paying four thousand dollars instead of six thousand, as was first demanded, he was liberated.

General Treviño went out with his army, intending to meet the enemy some eighteen miles from Monterey, but failing to arrive soon enough was obliged to have the engagement within six miles. The utmost preparation was made by the families for security in case the enemy got into town.

I understood more fully than ever before why houses were constructed in the style I found in Mexico. The walls are of stone, and a vara (33 inches) thick, and the windows are made with iron bars, running from the top to the bottom about three inches apart. The doors are of the strongest wood, and secured by heavy iron bars. The old houses were all built as securely as forts, but some modern built houses were a little less guarded. We prepared for the worst—we well knew that if the revolutionary party were defeated, life and property were secure only within our dwellings.

One of my teachers I had found means of sending to the United States soon after the commencement of the war, but the other I could not possibly spare, remained, and I placed her in the house of friends in a very secure part of the city.

The noise of the cannon was very distinctly heard, and the battle raged for several hours. At length, clouds of dust, which we could see in the distance, indicated that troops were coming rapidly toward the town. We knew not whether they were revolutionary troops returning victorious to defend us, or those of the enemy coming to complete their long-threatened purpose of destroying every vestige of the rebellious city. A few minutes determined, for soon came squads of mounted soldiers with the Governmental uniform riding into various parts of the town. I was not particularly alarmed until some seven or eight rode up to my house. Three went to the door and commenced pounding with a violence which indicated they were determined to make an entrance even by breaking it down. The others came to the window, and with pointed rifles, demanded " money or life." I had in my house at that time, a Mexican gentleman, our Protestant teacher, who had kindly offered to come and assist me in the protection of the house and property. I had also two Mexican boys, one fourteen and the other nine years old. Mr. Ayala, my Mexican friend, went with me to the window, and we assured the soldiers that we had no money, and as we were not their enemies, we hoped they would not harm us. But they were persistent, and thinking Mr. A., being a Mexican, might be able to conciliate them better than myself, I withdrew, and went into an adjoining room.

Soon Mr. Ayala came to me, his face blanched with fear, saying: "They will kill me if I remain."

I told him to take care of himself and I would take care of the house. My thoughts were occupied for a moment in the apprehension that he could not scale the wall, as the walls of our yards are very high; but I very soon felt the necessity of turning my attention to my own danger. The pounding at the door continued with renewed violence, and as my door was not secured by *iron* bars, it was evident they would soon be inside, if I did not do something immediately. At the same time the boys were crying out to me: "Do go, Miss Rankin; they have already broken the door." I uttered the prayer audibly, "O my God! what *shall* I do?" The thought immediately struck me, I will give them something to appease them; and as soon as possible took some refreshments I had prepared for an emergency, and went to the window in the face of of those awful desperadoes, who with rifles in their hands, I knew would not hesitate a moment to shoot me. At that very time, a man whom they had shot was lying dead on the pavement before me. My heart quailed before such a sight, and with manifest emotion, I approached and stood face to face, saying:

"I am **alone** and unprotected; you will not harm **a** helpless lady?" At the same **time I** passed **the** refreshments into their hands, which they eagerly seized; and those at the door came and partook with them. They asked me for some brandy, which if **I** had possessed, **I** should not have hesitated to give, even upon **the** strictest "temperance" principles, but told **them I** had none. They then asked me for water; and in attempting to pass a cup between the **iron bars, I failed,** as the width between would not permit. **Here was a fearful dilemma;** for I knew they were exceedingly thirsty, **as their faces** covered with dust and powder indicated, and **my** thought was, they will now order me to **open the** door, and in case **I** refuse they will shoot me. **I** stood in a maze, when one looked up **to me** with a **kind** expression on his face, and said, "Never mind, we will hold **our mouths** up to the bars, and **you may** pour the **water from** the pitcher," which I did, as one after the other came up to be served. Although it was quite a novel mode of waiting **upon guests, yet I** think **I** never enjoyed greater satisfaction in **any manner of** entertainment which **I** had ever before **adopted.** They became quite amused over the performance, and inquiring if General Trevino's house was on the other side of the street, they departed. I heard them break into **the** house; shooting the man who was left in charge, (the family **had left.)** They also broke and ruined every thing **they** could not carry away. By this time the city was full of soldiers, fully bent upon murder and robbery.

Four men were killed but a short distance from my house; indeed, every person, man, woman and child, found on the street was shot down. The utmost effort was made to break open doors, with axes and by balls, and in some cases they succeeded. In one of the principal business houses, a young man was instantly killed while at his desk, by a bullet fired through the key-hole, and penetrating his neck.

For four hours I was in the house alone with my two boys, whom I kept concealed lest they might be seen and killed. I knew none of my friends could get to my relief, and I greatly feared I might have to remain all night, and I well knew those awful creatures would become so much intoxicated by that time, that I should fail in my attempts to conciliate them.

About sunset the tramping of horses ceased, and the firing of guns seemed to be in the distance; and I ventured to look out of my window and could see no one either way on the street. I felt that was my time to escape, and told the elder boy to open the door, and taking the smaller one, I passed out, saying to the one I left, " Remain and take care of the house, and as soon as possible I will send some one to you." I hastened out. I had not been out of the house before that day, for a month, on account of sickness, and I felt I could only walk. I had not proceded more than a block toward my place of refuge, when the boy looked back, saying: "They are coming." I cast my eye around, and saw several horsemen riding full speed, with their rifles before them, about three blocks off. I thought I have passed through too much peril this afternoon to be shot down on the street; and I quickened my pace with a strength I scarcely knew I possessed, and succeeded in getting to my friends, who had suffered the most intense anxiety for my life. A sum of money had been offered for some one if he would go to me, but when the attempt was made, the sight of the dead upon the street, prevented him from getting to my house.

At dark some officers of the government came into Monterey, and brought the men to order. At the time the battle ceased, both parties it seemed, believed themselves beaten; and the Generals, Mexican-like, fled from the field, leaving their men of course in perfect disorder. Carillo, the Government General, ran and did not halt until he got to the Rio Grande, never returning, but was heard from some time after at Vera Cruz. Trevino, being more at home, drew up when he got about thirty miles, and after a little delay, ascertaining that he had not really been whipped, he came back next morning and took possession of the field, collecting his dispersed soldiers. Three colonels of the government being left on the field, and finding their general was missing, concluded he had gone to Monterey, came in, and finding the town in the condition it was, took possession. A provisionary governor was constituted out of one of the colonels, and a government was set up which remained in force all of five days; at the end of which time, General Trevino and his troops came in and took possession; taking the newly elected governor and thrusting him into prison.

16

CHAPTER XXIII.

Still in the hands of the Revolutionists—The people determined the trouble should cease—The Generals consent to
obtain terms from Juarez—Three men sent to the city of
Mexico—Juarez rejects them—His death occurring in ten
days after their arrival, Lerdo de Tejada came in power—
Issued an amnesty proclamation—Peace declared—Government troops take possession of Monterey—Mission
house demanded for Gen. Rocha—Resisted—Mission
again prospered—Obtained a competent teacher for a
young men's training school in Monterey—Thirty pupils
under his instruction.

OUR condition was not at all improved, as we
were still in the hands of the Revolutionists,
and subject to continued annoyances from the Government party, which, we were well aware, would
not give up the contest until Monterey was in its
possession. The people of Monterey, and, indeed,
of the whole state, were completely overwhelmed
with the attendant evils of the war, and the citizens, with unanimous voice, urged the commanders
to bring the unhappy contest to a close.

The pressure being so great, Treviño and Qui-
roga consented, provided Juarez would grant cer-
tain conditions which they proposed, and three of
the most reliable men of Monterey were selected to
go to the capital and confer with Juarez personally. Accordingly, they started, leaving Monterey

the middle of June, and arriving in the city of Mexico about the middle of July. They obtained access to the President, and presented the terms of capitulation offered by the revolutionary generals. The terms were obstinately rejected by Juarez, and no hope left that any favor would be shown the rebellious party either personally or in State matters. This was the condition of affairs at the time of Juarez's death, which occurred ten days after the arrival of this commission.

The death of Juarez opened the way for Lerdo de Tejada to come into power, who, happily, was a favorite with all parties. The Revolutionists had offered to lay down their arms some months before, if Juarez would vacate the presidential chair in favor of Lerdo, who, they claimed, had received more votes at the previous election than Juarez.

Lerdo immediately issued an amnesty proclamation, and in less than two months all parties became satisfied, and peace reigned once more in Mexico.

Lerdo was made president by a vast majority at the proper time for the election; and the position which he has taken in favor of the highest interests of the country, promises progress and prosperity. There may be, however, a remnant yet left of discord and revolution, and we know not how soon it may be stirred into hostile activity. Nevertheless, improvement is unquestionably stamped upon Mexico, yet she may still be subject to some drawbacks, but will, I doubt not, when fully sifted, become a nation worthy of respect. Public schools are being established throughout the country—good school buildings are being erected, and the general attendance of the youth is required. The future generation of Mexicans will, undoubtedly, bear the impress of the great and stupendous blessings of religious freedom.

I will return again to our condition in Monterey. About the first of July, Rocha, Government General, recaptured the city, and order, comparatively, was restored. Although we anticipated more outrages upon the advent of the troops, yet we happily escaped. The revolutionary generals, seeing resistance no longer possible, took the imprisoned governor, and re-instating him in command of the city, quietly withdrew with their forces and ordnance.

The morning of the advent of the Government troops, an order came to me for the mission house to accommodate General Rocha and staff.

Some hundred houses in the city were also demanded for the accommodation of officers and retinue. I was not at all pleased with the proposal, and was determined to resist compliance with the order, and sent immediately to the governor and alcalda for their influence in countermanding it. These officials had already left the city to meet the army, which was expected to arrive at twelve. Nothing could be done until their arrival, but we prepared for the worst, and removed every thing from the house, knowing that the occupants, with their numerous attendants, would not fail to ruin books, furniture, and every thing else found in a Protestant house, from mere recklessness, if nothing more. We informed the American consul, and he, with other friends, met General Rocha upon his entrance into town, informing him that the house was owned by foreigners, and occupied by American ladies. These facts elicited the heartiest apologies from the general for the mistake, as he called it, as foreign property is exempt, by the laws of Mexico, from military uses. The American flag, which I had on the house that day, was duly honored, and I was much amused to hear Mexicans say, as they passed, "Should any wrong be done that house, there will a bigger ball in Mexico than ever has been yet." We received the kindest attentions from the officers, finding among them some decided Protestants.

Our mission, which had been somewhat checked in its operations, soon recuperated, and our colporteurs were able to go out again upon their work. Our ordained ministers proved great helps, and we were fortunate in obtaining the services of a highly educated Protestant teacher. This man, Jesus Ayala, had been converted in Zacatecas, through the instrumentality of one of the colporteurs of the Bible Society, from whom he obtained a Bible, and with the instruction which the colporteur was able to give, he became a decided Protestant Christian man. He came to us, without any pretensions, and although he had certificates of character from Juarez and other distinguished men, he did not present them to us as recommendations. When I inquired, some time after we became acquainted with him, why he did not show us these credentials upon his arrival, he replied, "I preferred winning your good opinion by my *conduct.*"

We employed him in a "young men's training school," and he succeeded to our perfect satisfaction. He, with his wife, united with our church, and proved to be a valuable acquisition to the mission.*

---

* I regret to state that they have now left our mission, and returned to Zacatecas.

CHAPTER XXIV.

Failing health—Felt I must leave the field, **or soon** die—Bit-
terness of the cup—Resignation to the Master's will—Came
to New York—The **A. & F. C. U.** decline to receive my
resignation—Wished me remain **at** the head of the Mission—Finally left me to transfer the Mission as I thought
proper—Concluded to transfer it to the A. B. C. F. M.—
Accepted.

I MUST now come **to the** most trying **event of my**
twenty years missionary life **among the** Mexicans. The labors **and cares of** the **many** years
were developing consequences which warned me
that **my** physical ability for continued work was
very precarious. **A** disease, contracted upon my
first entrance into Texas in 1847, intermittent fever,
increased **to** such a degree, that I became **nearly**
prostrated. Also, a severe attack **of** sickness which
I **had on** the sea, upon my **return from** the United
States in 1871, aided greatly in undermining my
constitution. I had entertained the hope that **I**
might continue to labor, and **die on** the field. In-
deed, it had been the long cherished desire of my
heart, that **I** might make my last resting-place with
the Mexican people, and with them **rise in** the
morning of the resurrection, **as a testimony** that I
had desired their salvation.

Yet it was a serious question, whether I ought to remain with the impression that I could live but a brief time, or whether I should not put the work into other hands, and seek a more congenial clime for my broken constitution. The latter branch of the alternative seemed more consistent, as by so doing, my life might be prolonged for further service in my Master's vineyard. But it was a painful struggle to contemplate the abandonment of my long loved and dearly cherished work. How could I consent to leave those native converts, with whom I had enjoyed such sweet Christian communion—no more to meet them in the delightful worship of God's sanctuary? Never did those trophies of Christ's love appear so precious, as when I felt I must tear myself from them. And the evangelists, teachers, and colporteurs, how could I leave them and no more guide them in their work for Christ and souls—sending them forth and waiting their return with reports which rejoiced my heart?

Although I loved the work beyond my own life, yet there seemed to be a duty in the matter, and I carried my sorrows to my Divine Master, who, I believed, had put the work into my hands, and had been, during all those years of labor, my guide and support. In humble confidence, I was constrained to believe it to be His will that I should retire from the arduous duties, and surrender the mission into the hands of other laborers whom He might call into the field. The mission had assumed proportions which required ordained ministers; and it seemed proper that the general direction of the whole work should be in their hands. This consideration, and the failing condition of my health, seemed to be the meeting of two direct Providences leading to the same conclusions.

I felt thankful that God had given me health and strength to labor for Mexico when no others would condescend to notice such a hopeless field. I thought of the times I had turned and wept, because no one appeared to care for the souls of the poor Mexicans. But now, evangelical Christians, with one heart and one mind, say by their actions, "We *will* take Mexico for Christ." What a happy contrast! Missionaries of all Protestant denominations* are hastening to spread the Gospel among the long neglected people.

In view of these facts, my heart seemed relieved of its burden, and I settled peacefully into the conclusion that the evidently necessary change was in the order of God's providence, and in accordance with His own wise purpose. I arranged all matters pertaining to the mission as well as I could, and committed the oversight of the work to Rev. Mr. Beveridge, until permanent arrangements could be made. In the month of September of 1872, I came to New York to confer with the American and Foreign Christian Union, the Society with which I

---

* Several missionary Boards entered the field after 1870.

17

had been connected since 1856. The directors declined to accept my resignation, desiring me to retain the mission under my control, and do little or much, as my health might permit. I could not feel that any more missionary service on the field was my duty, yet, in consequence of this decision of theirs, I waited for further developments of Providence. I continued my solicitation for funds for the support of the mission as hitherto, until January of '73, at which time, the American and Foreign Christian Union became convinced that they would be compelled to give up all their foreign work, on account of the withdrawal of the support of the various denominations. The directors notified me of this fact, and left me to dispose of the Mexican mission as my judgment and choice might dictate.

I decided to confer with the American Board, in relation to the transfer of the mission to it, and in the month of March, 1873, I went to Boston and presented the matter to the Prudential Committee of that Board. I gave them the history of the mission from its commencement, with all the attendant circumstances, as accurately as possible; and after due deliberation they proposed to receive it, with all its appurtenances and responsibilities. Although I had full confidence in the American Board, yet, when I came actually to surrender my dearly cherished treasure, "the fruits of more than a score of years of weeping, and bearing precious seed," my heart again shrank, and I exclaimed, "How *can* I give it up." I left the rooms of the Board without being able to say, "I relinquish the mission into your hands," and retired to my dwelling—passing the night in meditating upon the duty which I felt lay before me. "About the fourth watch" of the night, appeared One, who in other scenes of trial had come "walking upon the sea" of trouble, and calmed my anxious heart. By faith I realized the sympathy of my Divine Master, and felt the comforting assurance that the mission was His, and that He would take care of all its precious interests. Indeed, I was made conscious that it was even dearer to Him than to myself. The next morning I returned to the Rooms, and with the full consent of my heart, gave the mission and all its interests into the hands of the American Board.

It was received with a favorable appreciation, and I feel confident that it will have due consideration in the future. I relinquished all further care and responsibility; the Board assuming the entire support of the mission, and thus relieving me from any more solicitation of funds. Four new missionaries have already been sent into the field; yet more even are needed to occupy the whole extent of territory assumed by the Board.

CHAPTER XXV.

Concluding thoughts—Points in Northern Mexico should be immediately occupied—True policy of treating Catholics —Deacon Stoddard's advice—Spirit of popery still alive in Mexico—Martyrdom of Stephens—Crowning joy of my work among the Mexican people.

IMPORTANT points in Northern Mexico should be immediately occupied by other missionaries, to collect congregations, organize churches, and put into exercise native talent and ability. Mexico should become evangelized mainly through the instrumentality of Mexicans themselves, yet they need to be guided into the best manner of working, and require a leading mind to direct them. They are very submissive, and most passively yield to advice and instruction.

Much precious seed has been scattered by Bible agents and colporteurs over a wide expanse of country in Northern Mexico, and is, I doubt not, destined yet to bear an abundant harvest. No means should be lacking for the complete development of this work of faith and prayer, and it is hoped that the American churches will not be remiss in their duty to sustain the hands of the Board with all the necessary means for carrying forward this work as its importance demands.

A church edifice has been in contemplation in

Monterey, to be built on a lot which I purchased at the same time I did the Seminary building. For prudential reasons I deferred its erection, although I have had funds for the purpose for four or five years. I have thought it better not to do too much at once, but wait until the public mind was somewhat prepared for seeing a *bona fide* Protestant *church* right in their midst, especially as the Seminary building was sufficiently ample to allow us a very commodious chapel for religious services.

I believe it wise, as far as possible, to avoid exciting prejudices in our labors among Roman Catholics. The tenacity with which they adhere to their religion should be carefully recognized, and every thing avoided which tends to vex and irritate them, even though we may defer somewhat to their prejudices. It has been a fixed principle with me not to attack their religion, but present the Truth, and let that do its work. To this sentiment, which I have found eminently judicious, I am indebted to a man of sainted memory, the late Deacon Charles Stoddard, of Boston, Mass., upon whom I called in my early labors for Mexico. After making me a liberal donation for the object I had in hand, he said, " In your labors among Romanists, be sure to make no decided demonstrations against their religion ; only present the Truth to them. If you wish to enlighten a room, you carry a light and set it down in it, and the darkness will disperse of itself."

The application of this idea has always been pertinent with me, and I would recommend its adoption to all others who are called into this department of Christian labor. While we are admonished to "be harmless as doves," we should also endeavor to "be wise as serpents." An appearance of timidity should be carefully avoided, and yet to avoid an undue presumption is equally important. With the Truth of God in our hearts and in our hands, we can afford to be bold, with a holy boldness; and in a country where laws are tolerant, we should avail ourselves of every advantage which the law gives in resisting persecution. The spirit of popery is still alive, as has been recently exhibited in the brutal massacre of a Protestant missionary in Western Mexico. The priests never did a more unwise thing for Catholicism—by this act Protestantism will, no doubt, gain a footing which might have taken years to obtain, as the spirit of intolerance thus manifested can not fail to ensure the execration of all the better class of Mexicans, and it may be hoped that means will be employed to prevent the recurrence of similar outrages.

Although we may shed tears of grief on account of the untimely death of our fallen brother, yet far more may be achieved for the cause which he loved, by his death, than could possibly have been by his continued labor. Martyrdom oftentimes bears precious fruit.

It is gratifying to know that another has taken

up the fallen banner of the lamented Stephens, and is going forward in the prosecution of the same glorious work.

Satan may yet make attempts to maintain his throne in Mexico, but only to find himself baffled and thwarted. The Bible is rapidly shedding its hallowed influences, and will constitute bulwarks against which the gates of hell shall not prevail.

To me, the crowning joy of the work in Mexico is the triumph of Divine Truth over superstition and error, proving beyond a doubt that the Bible is Heaven's ordained instrumentality for elevating fallen humanity, and for bringing back an apostate world to the allegiance of God. If there is one nation of people more than any other with whom I shall delight to join in singing the song of Redeeming Love in the day when that great multitude, which no man can number, stands before the throne of God, I am sure it will be with the Mexican nation.

"And to Him who has redeemed us to God by his blood, out of every kindred, and tongue, and people, and nation, and has made us unto our God kings and priests, blessing, and honor, and glory, and power, to Him that sitteth on the throne, and unto the Lamb forever and ever."

THE END.